Stories
From The Riverbank

Stories From The Riverbank

And Other Tales From Onaway

Clifford R. Roberts

Foreword by Bill Breed, former editor of *The Onaway Outlook*

iUniverse, Inc.
New York   Bloomington   Shanghai

Stories From The Riverbank
And Other Tales From Onaway

Copyright © 2008 by Clifford R. Roberts

All rights reserved. No part of this book may be used or reproduced by any means, graphic, electronic, or mechanical, including photocopying, recording, taping or by any information storage retrieval system without the written permission of the publisher except in the case of brief quotations embodied in critical articles and reviews.

iUniverse books may be ordered through booksellers or by contacting:

iUniverse
1663 Liberty Drive
Bloomington, IN 47403
www.iuniverse.com
1-800-Authors (1-800-288-4677)

Because of the dynamic nature of the Internet, any Web addresses or links contained in this book may have changed since publication and may no longer be valid.

The views expressed in this work are solely those of the author and do not necessarily reflect the views of the publisher, and the publisher hereby disclaims any responsibility for them.

Cover design and photo by Bruce Roberts

ISBN: 978-0-595-50836-5 (pbk)
ISBN: 978-0-595-61671-8 (ebk)

Printed in the United States of America

This book is dedicated to my family, those I love, and to the loyal readers of *The Onaway Outlook*.

Contents

Acknowledgments xiii

Foreword xv

Preface xvii

PART ONE Growing Up In Onaway 1
    The Hankey Milling Co. 2
    Elevator History 4
    Dick the Dray Horse I 6
    Dick the Dray Horse II 7
    Runaways 9
    A Cowpoke Adventure 11
    Depression Cloth 12
    The Gage & Kramer Store 13
    Onaway Trains 14
    First Train Ride 16
    Railroad Crossings 18
    Coal Trains 20
    Adventures at the Onaway Depot 22
    Pete the Crow 24
    REPEAT the Crow 25
    Bandit the Raccoon 27
    Old Report Cards 29
    After "The Big Fire" of 1926 30
    My Source of Personal Ideals 31
    The Easter Bunny 33
    The 1926 "Gum Caper" 35
    Quarantine 37
    Home and "Boughten" Haircuts 39
    Hoops and Hoopsticks 41

Stories From The Riverbank

Megs and Glassies 43
Taking Advantage of Sparrow and Horse 45
Halloween in the 1930s 47
Mischievous Halloween Pranks 49
A Babe Ruth Game 51
A One Million Dollar Wife 53
The Family Garden 55
Onaway's 50th Birthday 56
Old Days Winter Driving 58
Christmas Gifts 60
Christmas Trees for Sale 62
Our Model T Ford 64
A Driving Lesson 66
A Fishing Yarn 67
Sucker Fishing and Snow Fleas 68
The Good Old Days 70
Catching Fish as Requested 72
Fly Tying 73
Primitive Ice Fishing on Black Lake 75
Ice Shanty Days 77
Rabbit Hunting with Old Gyp 79
Thanksgiving Headshot Rabbit 81
Muzzleloaders and Homemade Bullets 82
Sledding and Skiing 84
The Last Bell 86
Ice Skating in Onaway 88
Granddaddy Winters 89
Wintering at the Old Lumber Camp 90
Blackberry Picking 92
Blueberry Picking 94
Rhubarb Cellars 96
Old-Time Jelly Making 98
Bread Baking 99

The Onaway Fairgrounds 101
The County Fair of 1928 103
Boy Scout Bugling 104
The Onaway City Band 106
Blacktopping 108
The Old Library 110
Decoration Day Visits to Gravesites 112

PART TWO Life On The Riverbank 115

Watching Birds Fish 116
Wildlife on the River 118
Otters on the Riverbank 119
Friendly Folk 121
River Turtles 123
Canoeing on the Black River 125
Log Jams and Portages 127
Refuge at Riverhouse 129
Floating the Salmon River 130
Dipping for Smelt 132
Tweed I 134
Tweed II 136
Contrails and Turkey Landings 138
Eagles and Turkeys 139
Nature in the Raw 141
Fishers and Birders 142
Camping in Pigeon River Country 144
Naming a Bird 146
Smoked Fish Flavored Raisins 148
Signs of the Season 150
Turkey Trot 151
Winter's Beauty Arrives 152
Stoves on the Hearth 153
Snow Adventures for Grandkids 154
Substitute Teacher Days 155

x   *Stories From The Riverbank*

    Mole Holes 156
    Fruit Trees Required 158
    Remembering Maybell's Flowers 160
    No Place Like Home 161
    The River Ice Breakup 162
    Observations of Flora and Fauna 164
    The Clam and the Water Beetle 166
    Losing the Township Dump 167
    Cranberry Picking 169
    Family Adventures in Winter 170
    Escaping for the Day 172
    Backyard Mechanic 174
    Typewriter to Word Processor 175
    Writer's Block 176
    The Card Game of Spitzer 178
    When the Game Changes 180
    The Car in the Garage 182
    Making the Most of Winter 184
    The Onaway Historical Museum 186

PART THREE On The Road 187
    Louisiana and Texas in 1989 189
    A Cajun Wedding 191
    Arizona, Texas, Oklahoma, and Arkansas in 1991 193
    Florida in 1991 195
    Louisiana and Texas in 1992 197
    Texas Times Again 199
    Arizona and California 201
    California Heading East 203
    California Again 205

PART FOUR Other Writings 207
    A Brief Look at Our Children 209
    Leaving for the Peace Corps 211

Letters from Twin Wells Indian School 212
The Gift of a Poem for Christmas 219
An Anniversary Letter to Idamae 220
Bone Marrow Rebirth of Ann and the Family 221
Reflections on Idamae's Homegoing 223
The Gift of Grandparents 224
Sentimental Journey—Second Homegoing 226
New Paths 228
Signs of Spring at the Lake 229
Reflections 230
Fall at the Lake 231
Zebra Mussels on Black Lake 233
Alaska Letter 234
Volunteering for Hospice 236
Flash from the Past: Cliff and Florence Roberts 238

PART FIVE Photo History 241
About the Author 249
Name Index 251
Topical Index 257

Acknowledgments

A collection such as this one requires the input of so many individuals. To name each one would fill many pages. I do, however, want to acknowledge a few key individuals who have contributed greatly to the completion of this project.

Florence Roberts has been a champion of this project since the idea was first proposed in 2007. She has sifted through materials with me and helped me decide what would be of most value for inclusion. I could not have completed the massive task of assembling the pieces of manuscript without her help.

I must acknowledge also the great encouragement to continue writing that I have received over the years from staff members at *The Onaway Outlook*. Bill Breed has been a great encourager, as have been my readers through the years.

Watching my children and grandchildren grow up and scatter from home has caused me to want to capture for them the history and culture of a world they can only know through these stories.

Finally, I would like to acknowledge the contributions of my son Bruce and his wife Karen, who have worked with me diligently over the past several months to shape these writings into this publication.

Foreword

You're in for a treat!

Always a teacher, naturalist, and philosopher, Cliff Roberts has worn many hats through many years. In these pages, he shares his varied experiences. From his youth, when Onaway had railroad trains and few paved streets, to his years along the Black River and then to his home on Black Lake, his stories will bring many, many smiles and probably a few tears, some of joy and some of sadness.

Early on, Cliff held positions in industry and served in the U.S. Army Air Force Signal Corps before entering the field of education. After teaching for 34 years, from classroom to administration, Cliff retired in 1977 and then traveled extensively during the winter months with his wife. The nomads drove ten to twelve thousand miles during the winter months then returned home to Onaway. Even while on the road, Cliff would send his observations home to the local newspaper, much to the delight of his many readers.

As editor of *The Onaway Outlook* for nearly twenty years, I was one of those fans who opened the paper and looked first for Cliff's column.

Enjoy!

Bill Breed,
Former Editor of *The Onaway Outlook*

Preface

I have always enjoyed writing and sharing my writing with those I know and love. I have had three major desires for my writings.

1. Since I was a teacher most of my life (still am), sharing some little known facts of all natural things (birds, beasts, insects, etc.).
2. Sharing some historical information encompassing my past, the Onaway area that my parents pioneered, and how my early years were molded by this northern Michigan area.
3. Sharing my philosophical approaches to family and those I grew up with.

Most of the writings in this book appeared in *The Onaway Outlook*, the newspaper of this medium-sized village. The feedback of my readership assured me that I was accomplishing my goals. I have also included here important writings from my journals, personal letters, and other writings given to me over the years by family and friends. All pieces included here have been edited specially for this publication.

Family is everything! How and where I was raised, went to school, and fitted into the local area and growing community have allowed me to bring you a wide variety of experiences in these writings. Hope you enjoy!

PART ONE

Growing Up In Onaway

Pictured here is the Onaway elevator, a central feature in the tales of growing up in Onaway. My dad, Oscar Roberts, managed the elevator for many years. It was our 'breadbox," we loved it, and we learned the benefits of hard, diligent work from it.

Right next to the elevator was the home where Oscar and Maybell Roberts raised their family. The house grew from an office of a lumber company that my dad remodeled by stages. He added lean-tos at the back to become bedrooms for all seven children plus parents, a second story for more bedroom space, and another lean-to for the kitchen plus the dining room. The house was adequate and became quite sizeable as elder children left the nest.

Part One includes articles about Onaway—memories from my years growing up here and stories about my family—most of which appeared in *The Onaway Outlook* between 1993 and 2005.

From the Riverbank
June 28, 1995

The Hankey Milling Co.

Growing up next to the grain mill in Onaway shaped my life in many ways. The grain elevator still stands, though the home where I grew up has been gone for many years.

Bumming around Petoskey some time back with nothing better to do, I decided to try to find the site of the old Hankey Milling Co. It was the parent company of the Hankey Milling Co. of Onaway. Old-timers recognize this name simply as "the elevator." My dad, Oscar Roberts, managed the elevator, and I grew up within a stone's throw of the buildings.

When I was very small, we visited the mill in Petoskey. It was located on the Bear Creek and ran on power provided by a series of paddle wheels. There was more to see there. Besides grinding grist and manufacturing laying mash, a high protein dairy feed, it also made a number of types of flour.

The Onaway branch sold white flour as well as graham flour. Early in the pre-Depression days, another product was added to the line. It was named Hankey-Pankey Pancake Flour. I'm sure this was before "hanky-panky" was a part of the vocabulary. Anyway, it could be bought as Golden or Rye.

The problems at the mill were many. Young boys used the two-wheeled delivery trucks (definitely restricted for bags of grain, cement, etc.) as race cars and pushed consenting passengers, often trying to negotiate the corners too fast. Many accidents took place, and with disastrous results! Tiny holes could be taped over, but more often the flour had to be re-sacked into new bags. Then too, the sliding doors were open part of the time, and sparrows came in to eat grain. The problem was that they also left their droppings, which too frequently disfigured the flour sacks. Little wonder that my dad welcomed young sparrow hunters so long as they didn't damage anything.

Hankey-Pankey Pancake Flour was a good product and enjoyed a modest market until Aunt Jemima came along.

Not on the Road
April 9, 1993

Elevator History

How does that elevator work anyway?

I received a great letter from Kathleen and Edward Kapalla of Lansing asking for more information about the elevator. Kathleen grew up on Elsden Street in the family of Charles Mero. Her favorite elevator story was someone (no names mentioned) calling the elevator and ordering two bales of hay and a bushel of oats. When the person at the elevator asked who it was for, the very quick reply was "a horse." Bang went the phone.

Mr. Arthur Stark operated a general store on First Street near the old Latter Day Saints church, and my dad, Oscar, clerked in the store. About 1914, Mr. Starks built the elevator, and as soon as it was completed enough to have customers, my dad went to work at the elevator. Mahoney Lumber Co. had a mortgage on the building for lumber used in the construction and claimed ownership in 1915 or 1916. It was purchased soon after by Hankey and Sons of Petoskey. They operated two flour mills and needed an additional outlet for their flour as well as a source of high quality wheat.

All of the machinery, grain and seed cleaning mills, grist mill, corn sheller, etc., were run by belts from a long, overhead line shaft that was powered by a 20-horsepower electric motor. It also powered the equipment used to raise, or elevate, the grain to the top, or cupola, and then dump it into the large vertical storage bins. The burr mill also made excellent whole wheat flour.

The name changed to Hankey Milling Co. in the 1930s. Oscar Roberts, Homer Roberts (a son), and a son-in-law, William Hayner, took ownership in 1947, and it became Roberts-Hayner. Later it became Hayner and Sons.

I was born in the white home next to the elevator in 1918, and there is a lifetime of memories connected with the elevator.

* * *

Have you ever noticed lately that some of the things you do either take longer, hurt more to do, are harder to do, or all of the above? Could age be a factor?

Mike Merritt was my sixth grade teacher in 1930, and one of us kids got Mr. Merritt (woe to anyone bold enough to call him "Mike") to admit that he was 28 years old. How could anyone be so old?

We used to say "25 years ago" and then "50 years ago" and then "60 years ago," and now I can honestly say that I remember things that happened 70 years ago. Am I getting old or what? I would rather think I am getting older, and I look forward to remembering things that happened 80 or 90 years in my past. Now where did I put my glasses?

From the Riverbank
October 6, 1993

Dick the Dray Horse I

The power of a horse can harness a boy.

Dick weighed 1,700 pounds as a four-year old, and at times as much as a ton. Docile as a lamb and jet black, Dick became the dray horse that Charley Henry used to deliver hay, wood, coal, chicken feed, etc., to the elevator customers in Onaway. How great it was for me to sit on that high seat with Charley.

Some years later I was lucky enough to ride beside Eugene Precour. I learned my only French listening to Gene talking to "Old Dick," as we called him. In later years, I was informed that the "French" I mouthed at Old Dick wasn't exactly accepted and may have had a degree of profanity mixed with it. Gene Precour later worked at Lobdell Emery and was one of the men killed in the Big Fire of 1926. Harley Malone took up the reins of Dick, and I rode with him too and picked up a bit of Irish to expand my "horse vocabulary."

Dick had one speed—slow. But he was also a super horse. I'd seen him hitched to a train car of cement and actually move it after it was "cracked," or started, with car levers. The levers were slid on the track in contact with the wheels. Then both lever handles were forced down by one or two hefty men, and the car would start to move. It was then that Dick could keep it moving at a snail's pace.

Coming home from the last delivery of the afternoon, Dick had another speed. While not fast, Dick really moved to get to the barn to shed his harness, get rubbed down, and have fresh water, hay, and oats.

From the Riverbank
October 13, 1993

Dick the Dray Horse II

This story is a continuation of the history of Old Dick.

Old Dick was the dray horse for the elevator about 65 years ago. He shared the barn with Bossy, our cow, and their feed was stored in 55-gallon, open-top barrels with a hinged, lift-up cover. If the horse got out of his stall, he would eat his usual ration of oats; but if the cow got loose, it was another story. She would eat chop feed (ground corn and oats) until it was all gone or until she could not swallow another mouthful.

What a glutton! And this was really bad news. We had to put a shoulder under her neck and make her swallow a quart of linseed oil. The trick was to rub her throat as we poured in the oil from a long-necked glass bottle. If she overpowered us and swung her head from side to side, it was an awful mess. Sometimes we had to start all over again. Eventually the oil resolved the problem, but Bossy was a slow learner and would repeat the gorging on chop feed anytime she got a chance.

The elevator eventually got a delivery truck, but it could only be used when the snow had melted in the spring, and its use was stopped as winter approached. Winter snow wasn't plowed but accumulated in the streets, and cars and trucks were useless.

The arrival of the delivery truck meant that Old Dick was out of a summer job, so Dad arranged for him to go "out to pasture" at Roy Riley's farm, about two miles north on M-95. Dick missed his noon oats. When there was not oats for supper, he would jump over a low fence and come home begging for a handout of oats. He would have to go back to the pasture, but an ample supply of oats went with him. He really didn't like his "unemployment compensation."

Eventually roads were plowed in the winter, even the alleys, so Old Dick was completely out of a job. He was sold to Vern Jackson, who lived on First Street and farmed some land east of M-95 on Twin School Road. Old Dick was really old, possibly 17 or 18, and was beginning to look bad. As Vern drove from M-95 to his home barn back of First Street, Old Dick would come to a full stop at Elm Street and try to turn left to go to his old home at the elevator. How sad it was to see this faithful worker in his declining years still longing to go back to his better days.

I don't really know how Old Dick's very last days were spent, and frankly I don't ever wish to know.

Not on the Road
March 25, 1993

Runaways

Fixing our failures begins early in life. Sometimes learning does too.

"The cow is loose!" This announcement was enough to send cold shivers up and down the spine of the kid (sometimes me) who had thought he had securely tethered the cow.

Bossy was a big yellow cow, and during the summer months we tied her out to graze between the morning and evening milking. A sturdy, 60-foot chain was hooked to her halter and secured to a round stake composed of a rear axle of a Model T Ford with the gear still attached. This gave weight enough to drive the stake into the soil, and the gear was large enough to prevent the loop on the chain end from coming off.

Lazy boys would sometimes tie the chain to a tree; or the worst thing was to "guess" that the train wouldn't come in on the siding that day. We would slide the loop under the track and hook it over a railroad spike. Doing so was tempting fate, but it was quick and easy. Sometimes the loop would slip off, but more frequently the cow would pull the chain over the track, and the train would come in the siding! After the train ran over the cow chain, it "parted company" easily when the cow pulled on it.

Bossy knew where the best cabbage grew and often made a beeline to Mrs. Martin's garden (M-95 at the R. R. tracks) or to Annie Young's garden. If Bossy wasn't immediately visible, one of us would ride the dumbwaiter, or lift, to the cupola at the top of the elevator. There were windows on all four sides, and one could see a couple of blocks in each direction. If we were lucky and could spot Bossy before she was in a garden, we ran her down, repaired the chain with hay wire, and tried not to let Dad know about it. But if she had dragged 60 feet of chain through a vegetable garden searching for cabbage, we were in big trouble! It usually took $5 or two bags of flour or a couple of cords of stove wood to placate the wronged gardener. The lazy kid was "on the carpet" and often had an appointment in the woodshed.

Bossy was tied out in safer places, with better knots for a while, but there was always that fear that someone would come running in and at the top of his lungs yell, "The cow is loose!"

* * *

Everyone's car was their "magic carpet," and our family's Model T Ford was just that. We could walk to most places in Onaway, so our car was pretty much a "Sunday drive" car. Dad parked it on a small hill next to our house so that cranking wasn't necessary. Just release the brake, push in the clutch, and it coughed and started as it ran down the short hill.

I was six years old and had watched my dad start the car often. It didn't look too hard, so one day I turned the switch, released the brake, pushed in the clutch, and wow! As the Model T headed for the elevator, I pulled hard right on the steering wheel and ran into a row of piled cordwood.

No real damage to the car, but then all heck broke loose! I learned a hard lesson and was promptly spanked; but I'm sure Dad also learned not to park our car on the hill, especially with the key in it.

From the Riverbank
September 15, 1993

A Cowpoke Adventure

It once was common for families in Onaway to have their own milk cows.

I was a cowpoke at three and a half years of age, but not the kind that usually comes into your mind. Bossy was a gentle cow, providing us with lots of milk, cream, butter, and cottage cheese with enough whey left over to help feed two pigs. She freshened in mid-June, and what a pretty calf! Dad took me to see the calf when he was doing the evening milking. Bossy was tethered across the tracks near some lumber piles.

I'm sure I was told to stay away from the calf, especially while the cow was being milked. But I just had to pet the calf. Bossy reacted violently. She lunged forward with lowered head; her horns caught into either side of my Dutch-boy rompers, and she tossed me into the air. Dad saw that I was apparently all right and was so angered by the cow that he grabbed a 2 x 4 from the lumber pile, and with one giant-sized swing, one of Bossy's horns was knocked completely off! I remember crying loudly and Dad picking me up and carrying me home to Mother. Dad called Dr. McNeil, the local vet, who came down the next morning and removed Bossy's other horn and treated both of the stumps. I was so lucky. One of the horns could have caught me dead center. From that time on, Bossy was a muley (a cow without horns)!

From the Riverbank
September 8, 1993

Depression Cloth

The Depression caused people to be creative with their resources.

I was looking at some heirloom quilts made by my mother when I recognized some of the colorful blocks and patterns that had to have come from the Depression days cotton material. At that time, flour and some chicken feed were bagged in cotton sacks with many bright colors. The material from the bags was made into aprons, underwear, dresses, and dish towels; small, leftover pieces were made into quilt blocks.

My dad was able to buy bales of cotton print feed and seed sacks that had never been filled with flour, grain, or seeds. What a bonus for women and daughters who came to town with their husbands. The women folk picked out fancy patterns and colors at the elevator. As I recall, the empty bags sold for about 25 cents each. What a lot of sorting over the pile, hoping to find two or three just alike in order to make an oversized dress or even bed sheets!

The elevator also had milk-colored cups, saucers, and plates that came in boxes of rolled oats. These Depression dishes have become collector items.

From the Riverbank
Date Unknown

The Gage & Kramer Store

Few of the old style general stores are still in existence. Here is my memory of one from childhood.

The Gage & Kramer Store was just two blocks from home. We could just walk from our home beside the elevator two blocks east, cross Lynn Street, turn south of First Street, and go about half a block. This was a small mom-and-pop general store, and sometimes we were sent to get some small item.

Our family was large, seven kids plus my aunt Nora Fairman, which swelled the number of feet under our table to ten pair. Most food was bought in quantity, plus we had so much home canned goods and the large potato bin in the cellar, so not too many things came from the store. We had a phone, so Mother could call the store and place her order. Since it was "put on the slip," there was no money to carry and possibly lose.

As we walked up the three steps into the store, there were barrels with crackers, cookies, prunes, and so forth there. Just under the counters were small bins holding possibly a peck of all kinds of candy, special cookies, and miscellaneous items for sale. All of these under-the-counter bins were covered with glass to let us see but not reach in to test the wares.

The Gages were pleasant storekeepers, and they would remind us after a while that it was time to take that Clabber Girl Baking Powder and head for home. Sometimes we would be given a piece of candy as we said goodbye.

From the Riverbank
November 21, 1997

Onaway Trains

Trains brought the world to Onaway and Onaway's products to the world.

Trains were a very important part of Onaway history. I grew up within 150 feet of a spur line and within 300 feet of the D & M (Detroit & Mackinaw) tracks. The Onaway Inter-Lake paper, Vol. 1, No. 1, published January 24, 1902, has some interesting railroading news:

> The D & M Railway has put a road crew at work in Tower laying rails on the Cheboygan extension of the road. A chopping crew of 50 or 60 men is at work cutting out the right of way on the survey towards Cheboygan. The indications are that Onaway will be in closer touch with the outside world.

In this same issue comes this report:

> The Onaway and North Michigan line of railroad which is being constructed by Tench & Co. under the supervision of Mr. J. M. Potter is about completed. The line extends about three and three-quarters miles north of Onaway and is owned and will be operated by the Lobdell-Bailey Mfg. Co. for a logging road. It is one of the best built logging roads in the state.

Onaway was already connected with Alpena, Bay City, and Detroit. My grandparents, John and Adelia Fairman, lived in the Thumb area of Michigan, and it was easy for them to board a packet ship at Port Huron, Port Sanilac, or Harbor Beach and then get on the D & M at Alpena to complete their journey to the Onaway area. My grandmother was a lumber camp cook and my grandfather a "chore boy," which meant cutting wood, bringing in water, cleaning, and helping grandmother. So Onaway was not as isolated as folks might think.

Here is a partial timetable of D & M trains at Onaway on September 29, 1907:

Going North	Going South
9 7:38 a.m.	46 4:05 p.m.
47 1:45 p.m.	48 11:15 a.m.
*3 1:45 p.m.	*4 5:50 a.m.
48 9:55 a.m.	10 5:24 p.m.

* These trains are solid vestibuled, though without change, connecting with the P.M.R.R. for Detroit. Coaches, cafe car, parlor car with electric fans, electric lights, etc. Sleeping cars from Alpena to Detroit.

From the Riverbank
October 27, 2000

First Train Ride

What boy wouldn't be thrilled to ride the train?

I need to hark back to the Presque Isle County Color Tour that took place on October 6, because one of the spots we visited reminded me of an event 75 years ago. The tour bus stopped at the D & M depot in Millersburg, and Jody Doran told us about Millersburg history.

Just seeing the depot brought back memories. Since my dad, Oscar Roberts, managed the Hankey Milling Co. of Onaway, he had considerable business with Millersburg farmers and the Millersburg bank.

One day Dad needed to go to "the Burg" on business and said, "Maybell, get the little boys ready, and we will take the 4:15 p.m. train. Why don't you pack a picnic lunch?"

When Arden and I heard these plans, we were fit to be tied! Sunday clothing on Tuesday and a picnic on the train was very special, as neither of us had ridden on a train before.

It was a short ride, but the wonders of another world passed us quickly, and soon we arrived at the depot. It seemed like such a big building. Dad walked to the bank to transact some business with the banker while Mother and we boys leisurely walked around the village and visited the hardware store. The time passed quickly, as we had to be back at the depot in time to catch the "mixer train" by 7 p.m. It may surprise some of you that the D & M ran five or six trains through Onaway daily, including a full-service passenger train with a Pullman car or two.

We were ready to board the mixer on time, and the return trip was in a very simple passenger car, as this train picked up empty cars at each station and delivered lumber, coal, and mixed freight. The most fun for Arden and I was to drink water from a drinking fountain using small conical cups. There also was a bathroom, and when we used the facility, we could actually see the rails and gravel ballast as we whizzed by at 25 miles an hour! The wonders of modern things.

All too soon we passed the crossing at the east end of Onaway and could feel the train slowing down. We heard the whistle that we were familiar with, as we lived just a scant 100 yards from the main track. Finally, the brakes made a squealing noise as we ground to a stop at the Onaway depot.

If "show and tell" had been a part of kindergarten in those days, you know what my topic would have been when it was my turn. We had entered a totally different world that day, and it was firmly implanted in my mind that I wished to be either an engineer or a brakeman.

Arden and I were so happy that our parents took us on this "magic carpet" trip. I wish the village of Millersburg and the community development committee success in their plans to acquire and refurbish the Millersburg depot.

From the Riverbank
April 2, 1999

Railroad Crossings

Train culture and hobos came to be cultural phenomena of the Depression.

Railway crossings used to be a way of life in Onaway. There were only three crossings that were in or near city limits: the one on M-68 east of town, the crossing that went to French Town, and the crossing on M-211 (old M-95). I don't recall if there was a flashing light and warning bell on M-68, but we were well aware of the warning bell on M-211.

Living next to the elevator made it was easy to hear the bell, and oftentimes a glitch would allow the bell to ring and ring all night long. The power to make the bell ring was supplied by a lead-acid battery placed 500 feet from the crossing. Wires from the battery connected both rails 500 feet on either side of the crossing. As a train reached that 500-foot mark, the train itself completed the electrical connection, and the bell rang until the train broke the connection again 500 feet from the crossing. It worked most of the time, except when the battery failed or the connecting wires were broken. I am reminded of these sentinels of the past each time I see snowmobile paths where once there were iron rails.

A recent rerun of a PBS documentary was about the days when a lot of men, boys, and an occasional girl were riding the rails, trying to find a better place and possibly just leaving home so that families might get along better with one less mouth to feed. I saw my share of "hobos" on the D & M line going either south or north. Going south made more sense because it was warmer.

At the very peak of "riding the rails," there may have been as many as 10 or 15 of them a day going through Onaway. There was a small "jungle" in the woods just back of the elevator where some would go. We had a water faucet attached to the back of our house, and my father extended the water line to outside our fenced garden so that water was available to the hobos. Mostly they were not a problem, but our dog made very sure that no intruders came onto our property.

Those were very troubling days, and as the Depression slipped away, the CCC first helped stabilize the problems. It may have actually been WWII that really brought the Depression to an end.

* * *

Presque Isle County Normal was responsible for so very many young women and men getting additional schooling and a two-year limited certificate to teach in Michigan rural schools. Most every township had a one-room school, and since the certificate was good for only two years unless renewed by summer school work, the turnover of teachers was high. Six of my seven brothers and sisters attended County Normal and taught in rural schools at one time or another. My brother Homer and I pursued teaching as a lifetime vocation. Slowly the Depression relaxed its grip, but most young people had to leave Onaway to find jobs in the city. A lot of us original Onaway folks migrated back, retiring where we felt comfortable, among families and neighbors of the past.

Not on the Road
February 15, 1993

Coal Trains

Unloading 50 tons of coal with a deadline builds character.

I miss the trains! I grew up right next to the D & M (Detroit & Mackinaw) railroad tracks beside the elevator in Onaway. The D & M had a busy schedule in the early 20s and was still quite active until the early 40s. A first-class passenger train with a Pullman car or two went north in mid-morning, returning south about 4 p.m. I think it connected with the Michigan Central.

At age three, I saw my first black person, who was a Pullman car conductor, at the Onaway depot. My grandfather, John Fairman, would meet both stops of the passenger train with a horse-drawn rig he drove for the Conover House. Hack drivers from the other hotels also shouted out their hotel names, hoping to get passengers to patronize the hotels they drove for.

A freight train went north to Cheboygan and returned south the same day. I recall a late evening train going north as well. We knew this late train as the "mixer." It spotted cars into business sidings that were dropped off by the other freight trains during the day.

Car loads of many kinds of coal arrived, mostly in the summer. Hard coal, lump coal, briquettes, and stoker coal had to be unloaded into the coal sheds or delivered to homes and businesses. I helped unload and deliver coal as a teenager, and the summer I was 14, I unloaded my first 50-ton carload by myself. It took me two long days. If it took more than two days, you had to pay a demurrage (fine), which quickly ate into the grand sum of $12 earned for the job. It was very hard work, especially on hot July days. Henry Gillespie was one of the few men who could unload 50 tons of coal in one day. Imagine $12 for a day's work. This was in 1931.

As we travel many parts of the country, the trains are still important. I love to watch them, and their whistles are still music to my ears.

* * *

I spent a recent afternoon in "Florida." Let me tell you how. A number of years ago I put together a makeshift greenhouse on the south end of my garage. I used thermal windows 4 foot by 7 foot from a son in Cincinnati, log siding from an old cottage I tore down, plus other odds and ends. It was heated by a bucket-a-day, coal-fired water heater plumbed to a 250-gallon water tank, etc. A real "who dunnit."

Besides being a good place to start flowers and vegetables, it is my "Florida escape spot" whenever January or February produces a sunny day. A plastic-webbed lounger gives me the feeling of being at the beach for an hour or two. So I think I have arrived at spring and none too soon. I enjoy my dual-purpose greenhouse as I "toast" and look out at the snow.

From the Riverbank
August 27, 1996

Adventures at the Onaway Depot

Who has time to wait for a watermelon to drop? How about riding sheep?

I have had some very nice watermelons even though they showed up on the market a bit later due to the slow growing seasons. Watermelons arrived at the Onaway depot in boxcars in the late 1920s cushioned in straw and piled probably eight or ten high. What a great day to hang around and watch the extras, or day laborers, as they carefully unloaded the melons onto horse-drawn wagons to be transported to the local stores. Possibly only 500 were off-loaded for Onaway, and the rest of the load went on to Cheboygan.

We small kids just waited as the unloading took place, hoping a cracked one showed up or one inadvertently got cracked in the unloading process. When it happened, a worker would find a relatively clean place on the unloading dock, raise the cracked melon to about chest height, and let it drop with a great thump! The workers would then watch the scramble as a dozen or more of us kids dove in to claim as large a piece as we could get our hands on. These were among the very best of the summer days for ten-year-olds. How sweet it was!

Just beyond the depot on the north side of the railroad tracks where the road crosses to French Town were the cattle, sheep, and pig holding pens. The farmers had to drive their animals to these holding pens (and I don't mean in trucks or trailers). Normally they stopped at the elevator to weigh their cattle. The scales area, about 10 feet x 18 feet, had wooden gates at each end. Only about a dozen critters could be weighed at a time, and this caused lots of confusion as the herd had to be split up in the process. The weighing gave the farmer quite an accurate idea of how much his cattle weighed, and he hoped he got a fair shake when they arrived at the slaughterhouse by train.

Often the cattle, sheep, and pigs had to stay in the holding pens over the weekend. The farmers would come to feed and water their stock, but after this was done and they had gone home, what a great chance to get into the pens and ride on the biggest sheep! We were too scared to ride the cows (too much chance to get trampled if we fell off), and we most certainly didn't even think of riding the pigs, so that left only the big sheep. We imagined that we were real cowboys on the far western ranges. I know we came home dirty and smelly and had a hard time explaining how it all happened, but small boys will be boys.

The circus also used that general area in those days, as the circus traveled by train. My brothers Earl and Homer had lots of fun stories about how they helped feed the elephants and carry pails of water to a variety of animals and a special time when a circus regular took Homer's hat. My dad came from the elevator and promptly convinced the circus hand that it was not a polite thing to do!

From the Riverbank
January 9, 1997

Pete the Crow

Nowadays families have dogs and cats and hamsters for pets. Here is the story of a more unusual family pet.

Pete, our pet crow, flew into the open door in the Hankey Milling Co. office, grabbed a shiny dime, and flew out without even a "caw." Here is how Pete came into our lives.

We had been watching a crow's nest in a swamp near where Harley Malone, Sr., lived. A long walk on the old R.R. grade, past Storm's house, and there it was. I was small enough and brave enough to climb the balsam tree and provoke the wrath of both parent crows as I judged if the baby crows were big enough to remove from the nest. This was the second climb, and I selected a real feisty one, chucked it into a gunny sack, and got back on ground as fast as I could. My older brother Earl gave me a pat on the back and took the sacked crow. The crows quit yammering soon, and we were convinced that they really couldn't count; so long as baby crows were still in the nest, no robbery had taken place.

It took a few weeks to tame the crow. It received lots of good food. When it showed that it was ready to fly, out came the scissors, and the long feathers on one wing were trimmed about four inches. When it tried to fly, it only went in a very short circle of about eight feet. Later Pete became tame, and his flight feathers were allowed to grow out, so the flight into the elevator office was fairly routine.

Our family, with the exception of my mother, enjoyed having a friendly crow for a pet. Some of the messes Pete made were not to Mother's liking, and I didn't blame her for remarks about that "dirty crow." Mrs. Yeager had no good words for Pete either. He would fly to her clothes line and remove clothes pins, so some of her washing dragged on the ground.

From the Riverbank
April 26, 1995

REPEAT the Crow

Our first pet crow led us to go after another one with an even more colorful story.

A few weeks ago I introduced you to Pete, our first tame crow. Pete was such an interesting bird that next summer we went scouting for another crow. We knew where to look and the right time, so it was an easy job this time.

We came to believe that crows are not good counters. Taking only one baby from the nest did not alarm the adults. But if two immatures were "crow napped," the adults would abandon the nest. This inability to count also could be their undoing when we hunted them in the fall. We would build a makeshift blind within easy gun range of a place they roosted in the evening. Then the deception began. Four of us would boldly walk into the blind area, and in just a few minutes, three of us would walk out of the area. As far as the crows were concerned, the blind was left empty, and they flew back in the roost tree. This was their big mistake in counting, and when the shotgun blasted off, there was usually a crow or two on the ground.

What to name this new black rascal? One of my brothers came up with the suggestion "REPEAT." It was quickly voted as the best suggestion.

For some reason, REPEAT imprinted upon my dad. Dad liked chocolate and often had some bits of Hershey bars that he shared with REPEAT. A night crawler was the only food he found that was better than Hershey bar bits.

Dad walked from the elevator to the bank every morning, and a strange procession started with him. Gyp the hound dog followed behind Dad, and REPEAT flew ahead of Dad, stopping first on Billy Beale's house, then on John Leopard's, then on Grant Strayer's, crossing the street again to Russ Hitzert's, and finally landing on the bank. Each time REPEAT would light on a house or on a tree branch near to the road, he would sound his raucous "caw-caw-caw" as if saying, "Hurry up! Hurry up!" He would swoop down sometimes to beg for a bit of Dad's Hershey bar.

REPEAT became like a brat of a kid, cawing and possibly saying, "I'm tired of waiting! Let's go." If Dad walked down to the Wright's Newsery, there was another wait. Sometimes an alley cat got chased by the crow, annoyed by the overly long wait. But then the trip back to the elevator came. REPEAT made the return trip in record time, only leading Dad part way home and then winging his way back to see what devilment he could create on the home front.

We raised about a quarter of an acre of potatoes, and that meant a lot of hoeing and later picking of potato bugs. REPEAT would join us, and believe it or not, actually picked lots of potato bugs, which he promptly swallowed.

REPEAT died an unusual death. We kept him all winter, most of the time spent in our barn. As late March sunshine started snow on the eaves of the coal shed roof to melt, REPEAT would relish getting in the drip (somewhat warm from running down the black roofing) and look like he was in seventh heaven. He came up missing one morning, and a search around the buildings found REPEAT's frozen carcass encased in the shower bath that he loved so well.

From the Riverbank
Date Unknown

Bandit the Raccoon

Even a raccoon could become a pet in the old days—until it was needed for someone's coat, that is. Here is the story of the fate of one raccoon.

My grandfather John Fairman lived in the house just north of the old Outlook Building, (now McQuaid's Laundromat) on First Street. He kept a cow and a few chickens. But this particular summer, 1928 or 1929, chickens were being killed and carried off, probably by a skunk.

So my brother Earl set a couple of #2 jump traps, and the wait began. Didn't have to wait long. The first night the culprit was caught; it was medium-sized raccoon. It was caught only on the right front paw, so Earl and Homer decided to domesticate the black-masked marauder. And, being at least as inquisitive as the raccoon, they decided to do something about the damaged foot.

Somehow they got some chloroform, and after putting the raccoon to sleep, they removed the badly damaged paw and saved enough hide for a skin flap to cover the wound. Their surgery was a success, and a complete recovery took place. But where to pen it up? We had some rabbit cages, and one was enlarged to accommodate "Bandit," as the raccoon was now called.

Bandit thrived on table scraps, and we kids caught frogs and clams in season to add the wild portion of Bandit's diet. Clams had to be opened for him because the loss of his right front foot. We often gave Bandit cubes of sugar, knowing he would wash it, as he did all his food. More often than not, the sugar dissolved before it could be eaten. Bandit never learned, and he instinctively washed the sugar every time.

Eventually Bandit got away and was not so lucky when he was caught again. McCreerys trapped raccoons (sometimes in live traps) during the spring and summer and kept them in cages until their hides were prime and it became legal to kill and pelt them. The McCreerys' raccoon cages sat just about where the United Methodist sanctuary now stands. Remember, this was the era of coonskin coats for college kids and the "in set." We heard that McCreerys had a raccoon with a right front foot missing, and sure enough it was Bandit! Bandit became a part of a coonskin coat.

* * *

I was privileged to have Miss Margaret Young for my English teacher during junior high days. She expected us all to do our best and be fair in all things. I recall getting a composition paper back with the word *airplane* marked wrong, and I asked why. Being of the old school, she said, "It must be spelled 'aeroplane'." Thinking this unfair, I referred to the dictionary and showed Miss Young that "airplane" was an acceptable spelling. I won the battle but lost the war. Moral? Don't ever prove a teacher to be wrong, especially in front of the class!

From the Riverbank
Date Unknown

Old Report Cards

What we choose to save can make us proud or humble!

Rummaging through odds and ends that my mom had saved and passed on to me, I found a stack of report cards from Onaway Public Schools. What a treasure of memories!

Grace Engle was my kindergarten teacher. Miss Olive Butler was first grade. I recall Miss Butler trying to teach us about proper food for breakfast. Oranges, bananas, corn flakes, etc. My breakfast was pancakes, pancakes, and possibly fried spuds, and I probably smelled of this hardy fare. But when the teacher asked each of us to tell other classmates what we had for breakfast, I became very creative and related that we had orange juice, bananas, donuts, and corn flakes. No one was going to report a more exotic breakfast than this kid!

I assume I passed from Miss Olive Butler and advanced into second grade with Miss Iva Dosie as my teacher. Then to third grade and Nellie Barnes. Special notes under conduct: Inclined to Mischief—Annoys Others—Whispers Too Much On the plus side: Shows Improvement.

Fourth grade was in the Yellow Building on the west side of the high school. Then came fifth grade and Bessie Smith. We had all heard horror stories about this grade, but I had a great time and wasn't tardy all year! Floyd "Mike" Merritt was my first man teacher, and he challenged and inspired us.

I have report cards through the 12th grade. The names of teachers blur, but I remember most of them. Dad and Mom took turns signing report cards, and with seven of us kids in school at the same time, it was a chore. We stacked our cards next to where our parents sat at the table and made sure a pencil was handy. No prizes for a good report, just a smile and a pat in the head; but bad grades weren't welcomed at the table, and some verbal rebukes often followed.

From the Riverbank
November 3, 1993

After "The Big Fire" of 1926

Learning to love others who are not like us is a valuable lesson, regardless of our age.

Onaway's history was changed dramatically by "The Big Fire" that reduced the Lobdell Emery Rim Factory to ashes in 1926. Lives were lost, hundreds of jobs gone, and the whole community suffered.

All of us were affected in some way or other, but the biggest change that I can remember took place a year after the fire. My third grade experience was distinctly different. The Catholic Elementary School was closed due to reduced numbers and loss of financial support as many families moved away. Therefore, a lot of Catholic students became a part of the public school system and, of special interest to me, the third grade. In our neighborhood, strong feelings separated us, and sometimes bad names were exchanged. But here for the first time we were in the same grades in school, we knew each other by our right names, and we realized we were all alike!

Immediately I knew that Harry and Floyd Kapalla, Orem Mero, Dorothy Precour, and others knew more arithmetic than I did. They knew their times tables up to the nine's, while we were struggling with the four's. Harry asked me if I knew the "gozinto's." Wow, here was a kid that knew the secret of the division tables!

We all became good friends, accepting each other for what we were and could do, and my small world became greatly expanded. I think back on how Nellie Barnes, our third grade teacher, was able to meld us into a group of kids who loved to learn and who also learned to love each other.

From Personal Writings

My Source of Personal Ideals

The search for ideals and role models is a universal one. This writing was drafted during my college years.

After serious consideration, I have concluded that the ideal character which I have hoped to emulate is not a single person but rather a composite of many persons. In order to better trace this composite ideal and explain the attributes which were selected from each, I have decided to review them chronologically.

I have little recollections of formation of ideals, except fleeting ones, before I reached the sixth grade. I was the sixth child in a family of seven children, and my father, being thirty-eight years older than I, was not a pal in the sense in which it is generally used. I looked to my oldest brother for inspiration in my early childhood. Dad managed a grain elevator, and at an early age I hoped to be able to work in his place when he was too old to work.

I joined the Boy Scouts at twelve years of age, and my Scoutmaster became my first great ideal. He was also the superintendent of schools, which stimulated my desire to do well in school. His wonderful English and faultless speech fascinated me and led me to try to imitate these characteristics.

The next great influence I can remember was when I joined the city band at 13 years of age. Our band director became my temporary ideal, and it was his pleasing appearance, friendliness, and helpfulness that endeared him to me. My natural musical inclinations were increased, and I worked hard to become a musician that I knew my band director desired me to be.

High school sports gained favor with me, and once again our band director, who was also our basketball coach, became a greater part of my ideals. His sense of fair play, clean speech, and clean living so impressed me that the fact that I was not too successful as a basketball player did not greatly perturb me.

After graduation from high school, I returned for post-graduate work and added considerably to my total ideal in the person of the new superintendent of schools. His well-rounded personality, his evident executive ability, and his personal interest in me placed him high on my ideals. I was then 20 years old, and most of my ideas and ideals were complete, so I thought.

A few years of additional school, two years of teaching school, and a few years working in war industries in Detroit added maturity to my thinking, and I began to realize what a great extent my father had played in the formation of my ideals. His name in our small town was synonymous with honesty, integrity, and common sense. His friends numbered more than those of any other person in the entire community. His active part in civic affairs brought a note of pride to me, and his personal morals and habits were so far above reproach that I realized that I had been seeing in others that which had existed in my father all those years.

By combining the fine ideals of all of these men, I have a composite which will always keep me struggling to attain. At first I believed that I wanted to change to be like my ideals, but since high school, I have become more introspective and egotistical and have entertained the opinion that I see in myself some of the qualities and possibilities that my ideals possess. Freedom from want, religious tolerance and participation, public recognition and civic participation, stimulating profession, happy home, and wonderful children are all embodied in my composite ideal, and my ambition throughout life will be the attainment of these ideals.

From the Riverbank
Date Unknown

The Easter Bunny

All of us have differing recollections of our very early Easter Bunny, jelly beans, and colored eggs. My first Easter Bunny was a bit different.

An escaped black-and-white rabbit lived under our front porch. Our old dog Gyp would half-heartedly chase the rabbit under the porch, but it was safe there. One year as Easter approached, my sisters Ruth and Vera decided to make Easter especially fun for our family's last believers of the Easter Bunny. I was three and a half, and Arden was two years old. Our sisters built an oversized nest of choice alfalfa hay and loaded it with colored hen eggs. Nothing could shake our faith in the Easter Bunny when we found this nest and the black-and-white rabbit nibbling on the alfalfa. How great it was!

* * *

I was born in the white house next to the elevator, and there were some disadvantages living so close to where Dad worked. Farmers would drop off their grist and return to pick it up after closing hours. Dad or some of us would have to go back to get it. "And Oscar, I also need …" was not uncommon.

A family that bought animal hides and lived next to the theater in town could be counted on for interrupting our late Saturday evening meal in quest of salt. I can still hear the lady of the family pleading, "I need salt. My hide, it rot." There were lots of times my dad wished her hide would rot!

We kids got an expanded vocabulary just because we were so close to the elevator and heard so much. Were you ever in an anchored boat or on a dock when a boat with a loud motor approached? Well, same thing. Barnyard language, foul or fowl, reached our tender ears. Saturday on the town and a visit at a few of the 'watering holes' by customers added strength and spice to the very loud conversations. We were in big trouble if we either repeated what we heard or asked questions about their conversations.

Not on the Road
Date Unknown

The 1926 "Gum Caper"

Life lessons can be learned from childhood folly as well as wise words and examples from our elders.

Jim Snody has been one of my closest friends since childhood. I vividly recall the "gum caper" which took place during mid-summer of 1926.

Jim's grandfather operated The Snody Drug Store, and one summer afternoon Jim and I were in the back storeroom. I had never seen so much candy and gum! Jim said, "This is old stock, and we can take as much as we want to." So, filling our pockets to overflowing, we headed out past my house by the elevator, across the D & M tracks, and out to the big woods. We would unwrap a full pack of gum, letting the wrappers fall as we walked. Then cramming five or ten sticks of gum into our mouths, we would chew until the first rush of sugar was past, spit out the cud, and then repeat the process.

We went thru many packs of Teaberry Gum that afternoon, but Jim's grandfather discovered the loss. Since Jim and I were always together, he called our house. "Yes, Jim and Cliff have been here. They may have gone to the big woods." My older brother, Homer, was sent to try to find the two of us. His job wasn't that hard; all he had to do was to follow the gum wrappers and cuds of gum we had spit out.

We were surprised when Homer overtook us, especially since we had eight or ten packs of gum yet to go through. We got the feeling that we had been caught! I was left at my house for a later confrontation, and Homer escorted Jim back to his grandfather's store to explain the appropriation of the "old stock," unwanted gum.

This was one time I had all the chewing gum I wanted. During our teen years, growing up, and adult years, Jim and I would often reminisce about "the gum caper."

* * *

With winter almost certainly near its end, I looked at my woodshed. Big, empty spaces attest to the source of our winter warmth. But was it half full or half empty? My dad would have said half full, while Grandfather Fairman would most certainly have said half empty.

If Grandfather sent you to the cellar to get potatoes, you were supposed to get the most wizened, wrinkled, or sprouting spuds. When you fetched carrots, rutabagas, or spuds for my dad, you'd better bring the very best you could find! My dad's philosophy I liked. If you always bring the best, you'll always be eating the best. Grandpa always picked berries into a cup, needing proof he was filling something. Dad picked into a 12-quart pail, assured that his efforts would eventually see the pail get full.

So as I looked back at my woodshed, I had to admit that it was half full.

From the Riverbank
February 7, 1996

Quarantine

How do we handle the totally fearful? How does it affect our lives?

Quarantine! Just the word brought terror and apprehension to our family. The year was 1922, and my younger brother Arden had been diagnosed by Dr. Carpenter as having scarlet fever.

Since none of the rest of the family had any symptoms, all six of us kids ranging in age from four to twelve moved in with Grandma and Grandpa Fairman on First Street. Dad took his clothing and bedding to the "bean room," which was upstairs in the Hankey Milling Co. elevator, leaving Mom to stay with Arden.

Arden had an especially hard case of scarlet fever, and it seemed a miracle that he survived. Very high temperatures of 103 to 104 degrees dehydrated him, and he lost all of his hair, eyebrows, and eyelashes as well as finger and toe nails. Dr. Carpenter visited daily and somehow pulled Arden through this terrible illness. We kids could look through the windows to see our bother and Mom. Dad was able to put groceries and other needed supplies into the back shed, and the telephone was a real help.

I recall the quarantine signs tacked to both the front and back doors by the County Health Department. It was not unusual to see a lot of these signs when there was an epidemic of any of the dreaded communicable diseases. After the doctors had pronounced the patient well and the incubation period was over, everyone was required to leave the house. The Health Department then came back to remove the quarantine sign and fumigate the house. What a great time when the family could be reunited.

Our family had a repeat quarantine in 1926, but this time it was for smallpox. It was a mild case, and we all had a few pox marks. Later attempts to vaccinate me against smallpox just didn't work. After having been vaccinated twice in basic training, I suggested that the medics write to Dr. Carpenter to get verification that I had indeed had the smallpox. My Army records carried a letter from Dr. Carpenter, so they didn't waste any more time trying to get the classic test scar on my shoulder.

There hasn't been a smallpox outbreak for the last 20 years, and there is controversy over whether the last remaining smallpox disease (now kept in the National Health Department storage) should be destroyed. The native populations of both North and South America were largely destroyed by the introduction of smallpox by early explorers and settlers.

From the Riverbank
September 1, 1993

Home and "Boughten" Haircuts

Going to a barber to have our hair cut when we were young was a luxury afforded only in our teens.

With five boys in our family, someone had to learn to cut hair. My mother had so many other things to do that it was my dad's job to be the barber. Dad took his job seriously and really did a good job. The internal screw of a piano stool was fitted in the top of a medium-tall, three-legged stool. It was adjustable for height as well as turning a kid around to a better cutting angle.

Sunday morning before church was the time for haircuts. Any of us who needed to be sheared had to be ready. Hand clippers often pulled the hair, especially if a boy squirmed too much. A rap on the head with Dad's knuckles was the reward for not holding your head steady.

When you no longer liked how your hair was cut, you were free to go to the uptown barber—if you had the 50 cents. Charlie Rosciam charged 50 cents, while you could get a cut from Fred Light for 35 cents. If you didn't mind the sawdust and hair on the floor and the spots that missed the spittoon or a few rough places in your head, Fred was your man. If you needed an immaculate shop and meticulously cut hair, you spent your money at Rosciam's.

I remember an occasion when I had graduated from home haircuts. Charlie finished with a final flourish of his little hair brush, and when I still hadn't remembered to fork over the 50 cents, he beat me to the door and held out his hand. What an embarrassing moment for a suave 15-year-old!

Once when neither of my older brothers had the 50 cents, they agreed to cut each other's hair. Homer said, "I'll cut your hair first, Earl, then you cut mine." Earl's hair looked so horrible that he was waiting to get his revenge, but Homer refused to let Earl get close to him with the scissors, comb, and hand clippers. He waited until he earned 50 cents and then got a "boughten" haircut.

Idamae was always the barber for our three sons, and she was good at it. After I retired, Idamae cut my hair, and just last week my in-house barber lowered my ears.

From the Riverbank
September 17, 1999

Hoops and Hoopsticks

The challenge of creating fun can have wonderfully inventive results. Homemade toys make great homemade fun.

Hoops and hoopstick fun helped wile away the summer days in the early to mid-1920s in Onaway. We had all the elements right here.

The bicycle rim or "hoop factory" cut and laminated maple and beech to form the circular wheels. Special tooling took place, and spokes not too unlike those of today's bicycle wheels ran from the outer diameter of the hoops to connect at the center to support the axles. In the gluing and drying, some hoops were out of round and weren't good enough for the final inspection, so they were just thrown out. A pile of them accumulated next to the property line. What a find. By sliding under the fence, it was possible to select a few almost perfect round rims. Almost perfect was good enough for our purpose, so we stockpiled a few for trading stock.

Next came the hoopstick. Here again, the American Wood Rim Factory, which made the wooden steering wheels for cars, provided scrap parts that helped us make the hoopstick. Semi-circular pieces of beech, maple, oak, and even black walnut were cut and glued to produce those fancy steering wheels. An aluminum casting, or "spyder," became the hub to complete the wheel. They even made a "fat boy" model that hinged upward for those of large girth so they could more easily slide into the driving position. The sawing of pieces that formed the steering wheel produced scrap that we found ideal for our purposes. A piece like a skinny moon was fastened onto a round handle about 18 inches long, and we were ready to go wheeling.

Running behind our hoop and steering it with our hoopstick was great fun. We also used our hoops by putting a backwards spin on them. After a forward motion of about eight to ten feet, they would return to us on the backspin. Special colors on hoops and sticks added more fun and helped identify who they belonged to.

Using pieces of scrap from a local factory, kids could make a great piece of fun equipment. I haven't seen such a toy for more than 70 years, but I'm still hoping there may be some around. Would be a wonderful addition to the local museum.

From the Riverbank
March 12, 1999

Megs and Glassies

Competition begins very early in life, and the urge to win is ageless.

There is a special key on my word processor labeled Create Text. How I wish that it really worked! Mostly, when I am staring at the blank work area, nothing happens when that key is punched, and the space remains quite blank until some inspiration puts my brain into gear.

Karl Pregitzer and I were chatting about the most common topic of all, the weather, when spring slipped into the conversation. "Do you remember one of the real events that let us know that spring had arrived?" he asked.

I scratched my head and ventured, "Do you mean when we no longer had to wear our long underwear?"

That hit a common response, but Karl had something else in mind. "Don't you remember when the sidewalk in front of Snody's Drug Store was free of ice and snow, and the sun had warmed the cement enough that we could play megs?"

This is how it worked. Marbles, or megs, were made of clay. They could be bought at Wright's Newsery for about 5 cents per hundred. The glassies, however, cost 10 cents per hundred or more, depending on the size and colors. There was a special crack in the sidewalk near the front entrance of the store, and the cement sloped downward. We would sit down on the cement and place a glassie in that special crack in the sidewalk, and the other kids would roll their megs, trying to hit the glassie. The distance they had to roll from was determined by how beautiful the glassie was. If your meg hit the glassie, then it became yours and you took over the game. The kid who lost the glassie was able to keep all the megs. If you were lucky and you got a "boolyam" (a big bunch of megs), it was worth it. If you had a nickel and really wished to gamble, it went into the crack, and you could demand that the bowlers had to back up twice or three times as far.

I recall when I had a really big boolyam and some big kids literally picked me up. My hoard of megs was stolen by anyone close enough. I couldn't fight them all off, so I just waited until I had the chance to raid someone else.

We took pride in our marble bags. An empty Bull Durham tobacco bag was par for the course. Woe to the careless kid who was caught counting megs and glassies in the classroom.

Karl and I both relived those fun days but decided that we would have to wait a few weeks until the sidewalk would be ready to reenact those bygone fun days. It might be a real challenge to organize a megs game sometime later this spring. We will have to start getting some of the old gang who might wish to revive the game. But are there clay megs still around, and could we get up off the sidewalk by ourselves? And "ouch," the painful knees as we would kneel on the cement. Think about it, and we might have that special megs contest before July 4.

From the Riverbank
March 19, 1999

Taking Advantage of Sparrow and Horse

Young children are ingenious, as this tale shows.

We always used to hear the statement that "two can live as cheaply as one," but I'm sure they were talking about the sparrow and the horse.

Onaway was more than a one-horse town in the 1920s. There may have been as many livery stables as there were saloons. The sparrow was a nasty little bird, hanging onto the fronts of downtown businesses and making a walk on State Street a real hazard. The Hankey Milling Co. stored sacks of baking flour in a reasonably secure shed, but the sparrows were clever enough to find small holes in the storage shed. When a farmer brought home a bag of flour with evidence that a sparrow had found it first, the farmer's wife was anything but happy.

The sparrow population became such a nuisance that the city fathers enacted an ordinance that paid a penny a head for sparrows. This allowed a flourishing trade for the very small businessmen. The B-B guns and ingenious traps in the hands of ten- and twelve-year-old boys started to make inroads on the sparrow population. The heads were proof of population control, and a cigar box would hold 25 or 30 requests for money.

Summer sales were most lucrative as my brothers took the heads to the city clerk on the second floor of the courthouse. Weather was hot, and when the cigar box was opened, a real stench arose. "Well, how many do you have, boys?" Not wanting to poke around in the box to substantiate the count, the clerk accepted whatever number my brothers thought might be accepted. The sparrow heads then were dumped out the east window, and the clerk would say, "Here is your bounty, and will you take this stinking box out of here!"

A quick dash for the stairs, a run to where the sparrow heads had been dumped, and my brothers were in business for another scam game for a few days in the future. Adding a few fresh heads and keeping the box in the ice house kept this business going until the methods were questioned. I'm sure the sparrow-head scam never would have gotten very far if our parents had caught "wind" of the scheme.

* * *

One of the real fun things of winter was to hitch a ride on the back of horse-drawn sleds and cutters. As a rig slowed down to turn corners, we kids would run up behind the rig and throw the rope of our sled over the back runner. This was done with a good bit of stealth, hoping the driver wouldn't be aware until we were well underway. A fast stop was very dangerous, as the likelihood of sliding up under the rig was always present. Another concern was getting too boisterous, alerting the driver of the rig that there were troublemakers aboard. This is where the whip was used to good advantage, either to accelerate the horses, which usually scared us into slipping our rope and escaping to find another ride, or to convince us to head for home before we became the target for the whip.

From the Riverbank
November 1, 1996

Halloween in the 1930s

What everyone does just seems normal, even if it's a bit beyond pleasant.

Halloween was different 65 years ago. There was no such thing as trick-or-treat. It was trick all the way.

The once Onaway Courthouse no longer served as part-time courthouse, and city offices occupied the first floor. As I recall, the jail was abandoned and in terrible condition. The metal doors still worked but were no long capable of being locked. One year the big kids conned us younger ones on a dare to walk into the lock-up. A small stick then was inserted into the door, and they ran. There were some very scary moments until we could figure out how to get out of that moldy, smelly place. Another year maybe we could be the big kids and pull the trick on some younger kids.

Those were the days of dismantling a horse-drawn buggy and reassembling it on a prominent rooftop. At Mahoney Lumber Mill where Ellenberger Hardware Store stands, there were medium-sized lumber carts that three or four determined boys could pull and leave in very inappropriate places. Dr. McMillan, who lived on North First Street, had a late-ripening pear tree. I was one of a bunch of kids who remembered that and saved him the trouble of picking the pears. A narrow piece of cedar shingle forced under the bottom of house siding made a horrible noise when pulled back and let vibrate against the house. Obviously these were some of the simpler tricks. I can't remember when the treat aspect of Halloween came into being.

* * *

Early morning paper—a boon or a bane? The Alpena News recently switched to early morning delivery, and my morning routine has been shattered. My mornings had developed into predictable, well-managed time slots. Station WPHN provided the kind of music I enjoyed starting my day with, and then about half an hour with my daily journal, time for devotions, and snatches of TV weather. I'm not sure I like the morning intrusion of The Alpena News, and perhaps I'll read it later in the day.

* * *

To rake or not to rake; that is the question. The "neat-nicks" use blowers with long extension cords. Loud-barking, gas-powered devices do not catch my fancy. I could get my old rake out and clean up the lawn, but if I wait until spring, just think of all the real, natural, biodegradable nutrients that will have leached into the lawn. Also, consider the balmy days of late April or May when I finally have to face up to resorting to using the rake.

* * *

As the bright sun had trouble getting through to me due to dingy, dirty windows, it became evident that something must be done to clear up the situation. The windows screamed, "Wash me," so I took the hint and got with it. It didn't take as long as expected and has changed my view.

From the Riverbank
Date Unknown

Mischievous Halloween Pranks

Tricks on Halloween night were the norm when I was growing up, but this one taught me a valuable lesson.

Sometimes pulling off a Halloween caper takes a lot of planning, but the one I recall most vividly just seemed to fall into place.

A buddy and I were walking down the D & M tracks, headed to the Long Swamp one bright October day, when we got a whiff of skunk. It wasn't hard to find the source, a road-killed skunk on M-95 (M-211 now). The wheels in the heads of these two junior high boys went into high gear as we tried to think of how this windfall could be put to good use. Halloween was only a couple of weeks away, and who knows how we might have need of a skunk on that special night. We secured a piece of hay wire to a hind leg, tied it to a culvert, and promptly forgot it as we continued to hunt for partridges along the right-of-way.

It wasn't until about 9:30 p.m. Halloween night, after soaping and waxing a lot of windows on Main Street and having been drenched with cold, greasy dishwater from the second story window of Wright's Newsery, that our plans began running downhill. We offered to show some 5th and 6th graders the abandoned city jail cells and somehow managed to close the door on them. My older and wiser brothers threatened to squeal on us if we didn't release them, so you know what we did in a hurry.

Things were getting dull when my buddy said, "What about that dead skunk at the D & M crossing?"

The prize was quickly recovered, and we scared some girls as we dragged it around town. But how to get rid of a dead skunk? We were heading south of Main Street when a really daring plan surfaced.

"Doesn't the Superintendent of schools, Mr. Schoenhals, live up this way?" I asked my buddy.

"Sure, over a block and the second house on the left."

Before we thought clearly of the dire consequences of our fuzzy thinking, we had arrived at the house and knew what had to be done. Since it was my idea, I took the wire and, after making a couple swings around my head, let the black and white, smelly cargo go. It hit the side of the house with a squishy thud and fell to the floor of the porch. Before it bounced, we were in full speed retreat. I can't say for sure where my buddy went, but I ran for home!

The news of "the skunk flinging" got around school quickly the next day, and it was also discussed by older siblings at home. Then Mother put me on the carpet, saying, "Clifford, I think I smelled a skunky odor when you came home last evening!"

The cat was out of the bag, and appropriate punishment was meted out. I also had to confess and apologize to my Scoutmaster, who was Superintendent of schools. I found out that crime, especially bad Halloween tricks, did not pay!

From the Riverbank
December 1, 1993

A Babe Ruth Game

Looking back gives us a chance to see the truly historic events in our lives.

The following is a family story by my older brother Homer.

"How would you like to see Babe Ruth?"

This question from John Race fired me with excitement and anticipation. It was the summer of 1927, Babe Ruth's pinnacle year for home runs. I was a 15-year-old hero worshipper. The Races spent many summers at their cottage on Black Lake. John was a building contractor who drove north from Pontiac to spend the weekend with his family at the lake. Mrs. Race and my mother, Maybell Roberts, were schoolgirl friends when the girls lived in Applegate.

"The Yankees are playing the Tigers next week, and you boys (my brother Earl and I) can go down with me, see the ball game and the Big City, and come back north next Friday," John added.

We three headed south Monday morning. I was an avid baseball fan, playing catch, 'hot pepper,' and whenever possible, shagging flies from the bat of old Bill Van Loon, a local semi-pro player. Brother Earl spent his youthful years hunting, fishing, and trapping. Baseball was not his cup of tea.

As we drove downtown to Navin Field (now Tiger Stadium), Earl got up nerve enough to ask John, "Is there any place a guy could go fishing around here?" Instead of the gruff rebuff expected, John stopped at a sports store, bought Earl a fishing pole, line, etc., and dropped him off at a pier on the Detroit River while we hurried on to the ball park.

We sat in good box seats along third base line, and I could almost touch my hero, "The Babe," as he made it from third to home. When the last man was out in the ninth inning, I disregarded the "Keep off the Field" signs, jumped the low barrier, and streaked for home plate. As I ran around all the bases, a few field attendants tried half-heartedly to stop me, but they didn't have the motivation I had. I touched each bag where the Mighty Babe had touched and ran triumphantly as I made my home run.

"Crazy kid," remarked John Race, but his wry smile hinted that he wished he might have duplicated my home run.

Stepping ahead 66 years, the new owners of the Tigers have begun a tradition of letting kids under age 16 line up at home plate after the end of Monday night ballgames and run the bases. They bill it as "The Great Runaround." Shades of my past that took place in 1927.

Thanks, Homer, for sharing a part of my past. I was only nine years old at the time, so I wasn't invited on that trip.

From the Riverbank
January 31, 1997

A One Million Dollar Wife

Without measuring value in life, we can miss the invaluable.

We always look forward to and hope to get a January thaw. It makes the winter seem shorter and more acceptable. But you had to look quickly to experience the January thaw of 1997. I think it showed up on January 21 and 22.

Saturday, January 18, produced a low of -26° followed by a warming trend with some rainfall on the night of the 21st and then a whopping 36° on the 22nd. What really surprised me was the number of goldfinches that came to pick over the sunflower seeds that had been uncovered by the melting snow. At least 200 showed up! They stayed most of the day but didn't return on Thursday (which was a much colder day). Where did they come from? Where did they go to?

I'm sure that short period of time when the temperature zoomed from -26° to +36° (a swing of 62°) was all the January thaw for this year. And by the way, has anyone kept track of just how much snow has fallen so far this winter? I would appreciate having this figure.

* * *

I'd like to take you back 90 years and share some from my father's journal of 1907. This entry took place one week after the marriage of my parents, Oscar Roberts and Maybell Fairman.

> "I remember well what went on January 1st of 1907. Maybell and I were married at her father's home on the second floor of Harmon's Dry Goods Store in Onaway. My brother Homer and his wife Ella (Smith) Roberts 'stood up' for us. The minister was Rev. Pierson. Maybell's mother had a luncheon for us, and we soon after left for the little log cabin

I had built near my brother Charley's Cedar Camp, about one mile south of the south end of Mount Onaway, which is ten miles north of Onaway.

"Taking an inventory on January 1st revealed the following:

One brand new wife	$1,000,000.00
Our new home	25.00
Household goods	25.00
Cash on hand	00.00
Debts	00.00
Cash in bank	00.00
Total belongings	$1,000,050.00

"Our home faced south and was built of dry tamarack logs not less than one foot in diameter and eighteen feet long; the end logs were fourteen feet long, making a one-room home slightly less than 12' x 16' inside. A door made of boards and little windows on each side made it about the snuggest little home we ever had. A new sheet iron, air-tight heater, and a small cook stove at a total cost of $11.75 for both, and we could laugh at the twenty below zero weather outside."

Note: An unpublished collection of Oscar Roberts' writings called "Trail Tales" is available by contacting my son Bruce Roberts of Monument, Colorado.

From the Riverbank
May 5, 1999

The Family Garden

How is it that the pain of gardening as a kid becomes joy in our older age?

How long has it been since we have had any rain? I leafed back through both my calendar entries and my journal, and April 6 came up as the last time I remember rain. Daffodils and tulips, nevertheless, have made good progress. Vegetable gardening is now high on the agenda, and peas and onion sets could have been in the ground some time ago.

Memorial Day was always our family day to plant the garden. The soil was heavy clay, and even after harrowing, it still required lots of hand raking. It was a family affair; and with Mom and Dad and seven kids, it went quite fast. When Arden and I were toddlers, we could drop in big seeds such as beans, corn, and squash. Dad believed in putting lots of seeds in the rows, using the excuse that if the seeds were too close together, they could be thinned. Our carrots always were too thick, and they were usually very skinny.

Hoeing was what we liked least of all. I recall one hot day when we were teenagers, and our progress was very slow. Dad took the hoe from my hands and announced, "This is how to do it." He really sent the dirt flying as he hoed. But we noticed that after about five minutes, his face was flushed. He was glad to give me back my hoe, reminding me that was the way to hoe.

We lived out of our garden, and we approached every winter with a few hundred cans of fruit and vegetables stored in our Michigan basement. Thirty bushels of potatoes was par to last us through the winter.

I have rototilled more garden area here than we will ever use, but it is nice to be able share some produce with friends.

From the Riverbank
June 12, 1998

Onaway's 50th Birthday

Connecting to our roots helps us find soil to grow into.

I go back into Friday, September 2, 1949, of *The Onaway News* for this account about my father, Oscar Roberts. My cousin Grace Roberts wrote the article.

> "This year we are celebrating 50 years of life for our little town of Onaway. This is the story of Onaway's first boy baby. It was a husky baby boy born to Mr. and Mrs. John Roberts, Sr., on that warm day, August 19, 1881. The seventh child born to Mr. and Mrs. Roberts was named Oscar Adelbert Roberts. Oscar made his advent into this world with the help of kindly neighbor women and relatives. The nearest doctor was in Cheboygan.
>
> "Grandfather moved his family by boat and then toted the family goods by wagon and on their backs to the eighty acre homestead located one half mile west of the Four Mile Corner. He was a millwright and operated his own shingle mill with the help of his boys.
>
> "When Oscar was 12, his mother died, and their father and the boys kept Batchelor's Hall for a while. Oscar worked in a stave and heading mill for two or three years. (His first job was when he quit school at age 14 and worked in the woods.) He said his education was very limited as a boy, but that his wife has taught him a lot. Not many men will admit to that, will they?

"In 1907 Oscar and my father, John, traveled west to search for a new place to settle. They discovered the wheat fields of Saskatchewan (then Alberta), Canada. They liked the land so well they had to choose either Onaway or Alberta. The toss of a coin decided that they would return to Onaway!

"Oscar's family lived in North Allis Township and then moved into Onaway. Oscar worked for A. E. Stark's Elevator on N. Third St. He later managed The Hankey Milling Co. elevator, which later became Roberts-Hayner Milling Co. Oscar and Maybell had seven children."

From the Riverbank
January 17, 1997

Old Days Winter Driving

A look back gives perspective often lost.

Winter driving has changed a lot in the last 50 or 60 years. What has seen the most changes may be the car. Today we step from our warm house directly into our garage, sometimes a heated one, press the automatic garage door opener, turn the key, and we are ready to move out into the coldest and wildest that winter deals up. The ease with which we move from the warmth of our homes into the warm car lulls us into wearing clothing that will chill us to the bone if we are unfortunate enough to get stuck in the snow.

But this wasn't always the case. A winter drive 50 or 60 years ago was a really challenging adventure. Often it was necessary to remove the six-volt battery from the car at night and bring it into the house to keep it from freezing, so job #1 was to put the battery back into the car.

Car heaters were either non-existent or didn't put out much heat. When you bought a new car, heaters were not standard but an added option. Some picked up the heat of the exhaust manifold and could be deadly if the manifold leaked carbon monoxide gas. The cars were anything but airtight; even a Southwind, a gas-operated heater, kept only the driver and front seat passenger warm. As the Southwind kicked on and off, you could alternately get cooked and frozen.

A hand-operated windshield wiper just couldn't do it in the coldest part of winter. Standard equipment was a glycerin-soaked rag, drawn up like a small purse, with salt and even diced onions in it. Periodic stops (all too frequent) were required to apply this vile concoction to both outside as well as inside. More often than not, only a small, semi-clear spot in front of the driver could be maintained.

Often a number of heated bricks were put in a gunnysack and then wrapped in a blanket to provide the only heat in the back seat.

I remember a buffalo skin lap robe that was so heavy it weighted us small kids down, but it kept us warm to boot.

Roads were another part of the equation. Infrequently roads were plowed, with poor equipment, and there were the high drifts to tackle. There used to be snow fences that helped control the drifts, but many roads were closed, depending on the direction of the wind.

Tire chains were a necessity most of the winter. I can still hear the clatter of a loose tire chain hitting the fenders. A quick repair was required or else the fender could be damaged. It was horrible to lie on your back in the snow to attach or repair a tire chain with the ever-present, magic healing of some hay wire.

The winters of past years seem a lot worse than now and maybe they were. We didn't have snowsuits for children and adults, thermal underwear, or good insulated boots, so we suffered more from the cold and blustery weather. If older folks tell of the bad winters of the past, just believe them.

From the Riverbank
January 2, 1999

Christmas Gifts

An opportunity to spend time on a Christmas gift may be the best gift.

Christmas gifts for family members in 1928 were difficult to make or buy, especially in a family with seven children. Simple cards, hand-sewn dolls, jackknife-whittled animals, etc., made with the help of older sisters and brothers were par for the course.

Upon reaching ten years of age, we were given the opportunity to prove that we were able to cull beans in the elevator bean room. The bean room was located over the present office of the elevator. Farmers brought in threshed navy or pea beans; before they could be sold for human consumption, all discolored, split beans as well as stone particles had to be manually removed. A bean picker looked like a treadle sewing machine, and as we worked the foot treadle, a movable canvas belt brought beans toward us. Imperfect beans and debris were picked out and placed into boxes next to the moving belt. We were paid by how many pounds of cull beans we removed. It was hard work to earn a dollar. Then was the decision of what to buy with such a lot of money.

Another way we boys had of earning Christmas money was to run a trap line to catch weasels or ermine. In summer the weasel was reddish-brown, but in winter the hide turned to a beautiful white with the tail tipped with black. They were vicious predators, living on mice, voles, and even rabbits. Often a chicken coop was raided by night, and the weasel would kill chickens by cutting their jugular vein. Seldom did they eat the chicken but just drank the blood. We set #1 Victor leg traps and used rabbit parts for bait. A good weasel pelt would bring 75 cents to a dollar. (Weasels tracks used to be common but now are very rare. Up until last week, I hadn't seen a weasel for 15 years, and then one ran across Black River Road.)

After gathering all that hard earned money, Gumm's Department Store was about the only place to look for gifts, and it took a long time to find the right gift. We drew names, since there were too many family members to get a gift for each other. When Christmas morning arrived, a family tradition was observed about breakfast and gift opening. Neither breakfast could be eaten nor gifts opened until Grandpa Fairman arrived. I used to think he arrived late just to keep us kids waiting. It was his time to have full control of the family.

This past Christmas we were with children, grandchildren, and nine great grandchildren from infants, toddlers, and active three- and four-year-olds and a nine-year-old as well. They were the joy of the season. But this grandpa arrived early to enjoy all the fun. I was sure that toys were not bought from picking cull beans or from the sale of weasel pelts.

From the Lakeshore
December 22, 2005

Christmas Trees for Sale

The ingenuity of young boys must be tempered by the wisdom of their elders. Here is another Christmas tale from my childhood.

Christmas season was creeping up, and how could my brother and I make some money to buy special gifts for family members? How about cutting some Christmas trees? A great idea, but just where would we find some? I came up with what looked like a winner. We had trapped for weasels along the abandoned railroad, which was a spur from the D & M, and I recalled that there were lots of nice-looking trees of about five and six feet tall along this grade.

To young businessmen (actually we were 10 and 12 years old), this seemed like a wonderful plan. All we had to do was walk westward on the D & M track, cross M-95 (now M-211) after about one mile, and turn right on the abandoned spur grade that was used to haul limestone from the old quarry at the southeast end of Black Lake.

Now that we had the location in mind, it was time to put the plan into action. Let's see, an old hatchet, a rusty old handsaw, some binder twine, and sandwiches and fruit to tide us over until we got back. That walk to the Long Swamp was farther than we had remembered, and by the time a couple of promising-looking trees had been scouted out and cut, we were ready for the peanut butter sandwiches and the apples we had brought.

The walk back home was even longer, if that was possible. When we proudly set the prize trees beside our house, our dad said, "They are quite nice trees, but where did you get them?"

Confession time was in order. "But they were just there, and nobody would miss them."

"Well, what had you intended to do with them?"

We were a bit tongue-tied and stammered that we thought we might sell them.

Dad countered, "There are a couple of elderly widows on our street who might not be able to even afford to buy a tree. Don't you boys think they might be happy if you gave them the trees?"

We felt properly chastised and agreed that we knew exactly the two elderly ladies he might have in mind who would be happy to see two would-be Christmas tree salesmen come to their doors and offer them a free tree!

From the Riverbank
January 21, 2000

Our Model T Ford

Is the love of cars in our genes? An old tradition of families was "the Sunday drive." From these excursions comes the not-so-complimentary expression "Sunday driver."

A recent documentary on PBS brought back memories of the early cars in our family.

My dad had caught "the car bug." He wanted to see his very own Model T Ford manufactured and then drive it home. He went to Pontiac, Michigan, and his good friend John Race agreed to set up the plans. Dad rode with John to the Ford Motor Co. (Dearborn). After paying for the car, signing the papers, and so forth, they went to the assembly line, were told the number of the car that Dad had purchased, and followed it through the last steps of final assembly. The back wheels were jacked up, and the car was run for a few minutes to break in the engine.

Friction was bad in those days, and the car heated up, just part of the expected break-in during those days. The trip back to Pontiac required many stops to add water and let it cool off. The next day was a bad one too. Even with a very early start, Dad only got to Roscommon. The roads got worse and the gravel turned to sand in the plains areas, and it seemed that he would not even get home on the second day. In fact, it required two and a half days to get back to Onaway.

We all waited expectantly for the arrival of Dad and the new car. Tired as he was, he took all of us for a short ride after supper that day. What a wonderful thrill to know that Sunday afternoons meant going for a ride in the new car.

Some years later a used Studebaker came into the family. It was a big, heavy, under-powered thing that Dad claimed could hardly "pull a setting hen off the nest." It looked pretty good and was used to take the whole family on a summer vacation to Sanilac, Pontiac, Port Huron, and Tilsonburg (Canada). That was "the big trip" for our family.

The Model T remained in the family, and my older brothers could use it if they would take care of it. When Dad inspected it one summer day and found a flat tire, oil dangerously low, and no water in the radiator, he immediately sold it to someone who really had an appreciation for a good used car.

A succession of cars came and went. A grand Buick was bought from Ed McClutchey, followed by a used Ford purchased from Scrib Valley. He was the ultimate fast-talking, used car salesman, and Dad admitted that he had been taken royally! Finally, a brand new 1938 Ford was followed by our first Chevrolet. When I was given permission to drive at age 14, there was only the old Model T Ford available, but it took me and some of my fishing buddies to the Chain Lakes and some remote trout streams.

I'm sure I have missed some of the family cars, but in 50 years, there were quite a few. Now the cars I have personally owned would be a long list as well. The American male has had a love affair with cars, and it will continue into the future.

From the Riverbank
November 10, 1993

A Driving Lesson

Now here's a lesson on what not to do when someone is learning to drive!

Even girls learned to drive cars back in the mid 1920s. My sister Ruth had almost mastered the skills of driving when she asked my Aunt Nora Fairman and another friend to take a spin uptown. Arden and I, about four and six years old, heard the plans and decided to get in on the party. We sneaked into the back seat of the Model T and covered ourselves with a blanket.

It was a very jerky start, and the stop at State Street was a disaster. But Ruth got the car headed east, and before long we were beyond Glasier's corner. By this time, Arden and I had crawled from under the blanket to add to the woes of the driver. Where could Ruth turn the car around? The only practical solution the three teenage girls could come up with was to drive to the Y at Millersburg. Ruth was able to handle the turnaround at the Y, and the homeward trip became a fun ride, especially making it to the top of the Rainy Hill without having to clutch into second gear.

It was a ride I'll never forget, and I bet the same for my sister Ruth. She had some creative explaining as to why it took so long to give Nora and friend a ride uptown. Our parents were worried and just couldn't figure where Arden and I had disappeared to for a while on that Sunday afternoon. I think Ruth got some lessons on how to turn the car around without driving to Millersburg to do it.

From the Riverbank
October 27, 1993

A Fishing Yarn

Images of Tom Sawyer and Huck Finn were not created solely by Samuel Clemens; they are as natural as boys.

My brother Homer visited this week and shared a fishing yarn of some 70 years ago. Our oldest brother Earl was the real fisherman of the family, but my parents thought ten years of age was a bit too young to go off by himself, so he had to put up with Homer going with him. They would walk the railroad tracks from our home to Tower and fish in the Bowen's Creek where it entered Tower Pond. (I always thought that they went to Bone Creek.) They had a time deadline to meet, the 4 p.m. D & M back to Onaway. The fare was eight cents each. What a sight they must have been, two ragamuffin kids with their short cane poles, lunch box, and quite often some nice trout and bass to show to the others on the passenger train. Passengers sure got a good look at rustic kids having a good time.

* * *

A bit of rural Americana unfolded Friday afternoon as the Presque Isle Electric Co-Op held the annual meeting at the Posen School. This was an opportunity to meet friends from this big area that the Co-Op covers. The meeting was a 90 percent senior citizen gathering, but the formula they set up was foolproof: 1) a good noon meal prepared only as Posen women can do; 2) a few giveaways such as a nice, new yardstick and a small carryall bag; 3) some good music and a constant supply of "pun-skies" (I know this isn't the way they spell it, but it is the best I can do); and 4) drawings for many door prizes. You probably noticed that I didn't say anything about reports, election, etc. The really important things have already been mentioned. I met many old friends, and it felt that I had been at a family reunion.

Not on the Road
April 21, 1993

Sucker Fishing and Snow Fleas

Fishing is one of my greatest childhood memories.

"The suckers are running!"

This exciting announcement was made at the supper table by my brother Earl in late April of 1928. It really got the attention of all but the girls of the family.

"Can we go yet today?" we asked.

"Get all your stuff together, dig a bunch of worms, and we'll go about 5:30 p.m. tomorrow," my dad said.

We were ready shortly after school was out with three or four cans of worms, hooks, lines, and sinkers (an assortment of old spark plugs, small bolts, and rusty nails). Mother had packed a bushel basket of supper things. There were five boys with big appetites plus Mom and Dad. The few cane poles we had were tied to the Model T, and we haunted the car waiting for Dad to get home from work. One of the older boys had to milk the cow early, as we would be home too late. My sisters were glad to stay at home. As soon as Dad showed up, we headed for the High Banks above the Red Bridge.

The first chore was to gather lots of wood for the supper fire and bonfire that would burn into the night. While Mom got supper ready, we cut some long, slender maple saplings for fishing poles and rigged them. We younger boys made a few runs and tumbles down the steep sand bank, hoping we would stop before we hit the water. Some of the lines were baited and set out before we heard, "Halloo! Come and get it!"

The seven of us made short work of the baked beans, fried onions in potatoes, and lots of Mom's warm homemade bread. There was a gallon pail of freshly brewed coffee and milk for us younger boys.

Our feast got interrupted by a "Hey, there's fish on one of the poles." While Dad helped Mom put away the supper things, we got into the business of catching suckers. They seemed to bite better as it got darker.

By 10 o'clock Dad said, "Wrap 'em up, boys. Tomorrow is a school day." Reluctantly we wound up our lines around the poles, carried our dozen or so suckers up the steep sand bank, and headed for home. As usual, my younger brother Arden and I were sound asleep long before we got home.

I'll always remember and treasure the fun sucker fishing times at the High Banks!

* * *

"There weren't as many snow fleas as usual this winter." I knew this comment would get the attention of our down state visitors.

"Snow fleas? What a tall tale; you surely are putting us on."

"No." I explained that some warm days in late February or March our cross county ski trails were almost black with them. The visitors were sure I was telling tall tales.

Actually snow fleas are rather common in winter and are always thickest in or near jack pine thickets. They belong to a group of wingless insects called springtails, with the scientific moniker of *Colembola*. They move by jumping; hence, the term *flea*. They spend most of their lives in trees, but they come down on sunny days to eat the microscopic algae and bacteria on snow. They lay their eggs in tree duff, and hatchlings help make organic material as they eat the grass and tree droppings. So if someone talks about snow fleas, yes, they really do exist.

From the Riverbank
November 22, 1996

The Good Old Days

Who among us doesn't fall prey to the joy of embellishing "the good old days"?

My good friend Bob took me to task after reading from my column last week.

"Tell me, Cliff, what is so very great about your so-called 'good old days'? It seems to me that the hard work, drudgery of wood gathering, and the additional dust and dirt within your house could have been anything but good old days!"

Bob had me in a corner, and I had to think about what he had said. Good point, and if I had been back on the Onaway High School Debate Team (1936-37), I would have had to concede defeat on that argument.

We all have heard the stories of hardships of walking three or four miles in the cold of winter just to get to school. And then there was the return trudge as well. Of course, the snow was much deeper then, and every quarter of a mile qualified for as much as a mile. I think those of the older generation look at how much easier our children and grandchildren have it, and we like to exaggerate all of the details and then add insult to the story by claiming that we were tougher, more dedicated than others.

Bob, I "give" and will be less inclined to brag about the good old days.

* * *

Leafing through some notes on wildflowers, I came across a reference to weeds. It seems that if we cultivate plants that produce blooms that we enjoy, we call them flowers and give them special names like pansy, phlox, rose, and tulip. But what about flowers that are not cultivated and grow in places that either we don't want them to grow or grow just in profusion along the roadside or, heaven forbid, grow in our lawns? Weed is the name we use for them, and somehow we think of them in lesser terms. That brings up my philosophical question, or perhaps a statement. When is a weed a weed?

Roadsides and especially ditches seem to be covered by weeds of some sort from early spring until late fall. Are they only weeds? I have quite recently become interested in compiling a list of these "special flowers." After all the years that one lists birds, there comes a time that it is highly unlikely that one will expand the life list; that is, unless one goes to exotic places. But even then, the tropical-like borders of Texas can only yield so many new ones. But with wildflowers, it is so very different. Most any time that I carefully look at weeds in my yard, it is possible to come up with many new faces.

Bergamot, a member of the mint family, is a recent name added to my list. Frankly I am very happy to know this beautiful lavender-pink flower with a heady and distinct odor to remember. Now I consider it a lasting friend.

Discovering more of these weeds will be a goal when they next appear. Beauty is in the eye and nostril of the beholder. I must wait until spring, summer, and fall to make more of them my friends.

From the Riverbank
Date Unknown

Catching Fish as Requested

It's great to go fishing, but reaching the goal set for us by parents is a greater reward.

Once Clarence and I were going fishing and we asked Mom what kind of fish she would like. "You can bring back a nice big walleye and a northern pike." We had ours goal, and we came back with two very large walleyes and a monster pike. Now those were the "good old days." How very happy we were, and Mom showered us with praise.

* * *

Many early times at Black Lake were spent in our gigantic tent. When Onaway's concrete streets were poured, contractors bought vast amounts of canvas to protect against anticipated rain. A drier than normal time made hundreds of yards of new canvas available at very cheap prices. My dad bought enough to build a 12' x 20' tent with quite high sidewalls. Camping on Rainy Beach was the greatest.

From the Riverbank
March 22, 2002

Fly Tying

Fishing was such an important part of growing up in Onaway. The AuSable sparked the idea of the Holy Grail in northern Michigan. Since my brother Clarence was "big time" into flies, I too spent time out on the northern branch as well as the main stream of the AuSable and also canoed most of its length.

A recent article in "Country Lines" caught my eye. Bob Smock wrote of "Veteran AuSable Fly Tyers." I assumed that any history of AuSable fly tying would have to include my brother Clarence's part—and it did. Bob Smock wrote:

> One of the masters of this craft was Clarence Roberts. He was among the best fly tyers that came out of the AuSable area. He put several of his children through college by tying and selling flies. Just how many flies did he tie and sell? Five hundred dozen or so each year! This adds up to a couple of dozen per day, seven days a week, and 52 weeks per year. This after-hour activity was in addition to 32 years as a Michigan Conservation Officer in the north half of Crawford County. Among Roberts' best known patterns were Hatching Mayfly, Michigan Mayfly (Hex), and Roberts Yellow Drake.

I had some small part in my brother's start in fly tying. In the late 30s, I bought "the whole nine yards" of fly tying equipment from Herters Catalog and collected local feathers and fur. When I joined the Armed Services, I gave Clarence all of my equipment. The rest is history.

After the service time, I continued to tie some flies, but I didn't have the skill or patience of my brother. When my boys became interested in fishing, we switched to pan fish, suckers, and gradually to pike. When the ultralight spin casting equipment became available, I mostly gave up the fly rod and tying flies. I still have a few of the original flies my brother tied and will keep them as mementos of his contribution to trout fishing in Michigan.

From the Lakeshore
January 8, 2004

Primitive Ice Fishing on Black Lake

Seasons are a gift, as is gumption.

Sixty-five years ago Eddie Goupell and I did some primitive ice fishing on the Chain Lakes. We couldn't take a fish shanty to where we wished to fish, so we each carried in a couple of heavy blankets. After locating a likely looking spot, we chopped holes in the ice and then cut four cedar poles about five feet long and about an inch in diameter. Setting up the poles in the shape of a wigwam, we draped the blankets tightly to the poles, sat down on cedar boughs, grasped our spears, and the wait for a northern pike began.

We usually were lucky enough to spear one or two pike. It wasn't easy to get a fish up through the hole, and the pile of boughs didn't always keep us dry. I remember seeing one of the largest northern pike ever slide slowly into the hole. I truly got "buck fever" and couldn't drop the spear at this whopper.

When we had a few fish or whenever we got too cold, it was time to go home. Snowshoes were our transportation up the hill and to where Eddie had parked the old Pontiac. We were warmed up trudging up the hill with our small sled loaded with spears, blankets, and a fish or two. What a fun way to spend a winter afternoon.

The Pontiac started okay, and then was the 20-mile ride home, trying to keep snow and ice from the windshield and soaking up some heat from the primitive car heater. I doubt if we could do it today, a couple of upper-80s old "has-beens." But we can spin yarns about the good old times!

* * *

There is always some speculation as to when the ice breaks up as well as when it freezes on Black Lake. A professor from the Finger Lake area of New York State, Dr. Ken Stewart, calls Florence to determine these dates. It seems there is a close correlation between lakes in our area of Michigan's Northern Lower Peninsula and the Finger Lakes of New York State.

Florence has kept track of these dates for over 30 years, and she calls Black Lake residents to help in this determination. The shape of the lake is such that one cannot see all areas; hence, the need for calling Bob Marshall on the Bluff, Jim Henry, and others to be able to give Professor Stewart the correct data.

Early checking suggested that the lake froze over on December 26, but strong winds broke up the ice, and warming days kept the lake free of ice for another week. Then the "deep freeze" set in with a vengeance, and Black Lake was frozen. This is not to say that the ice is safe in all places, so just be careful!

From the Lakeshore
May 5, 2005

Ice Shanty Days

Invention is the mother of adventure.

The ice was four inches thick, and now was the time to try out my shanty. In 1938 there were no folding ice shanties, and I had put together a strange contraption. The frame was 2 x 2 pine; the object was to keep it as light as I could. It was 30 inches wide and 60 inches high and 70 inches long. I braced it inside and covered the outside with reinforced building paper that was waterproof. The seat was opposite the door, and longitudinal 2 x 2s were place so that once I had entered the shanty, it could be picked up and carried. No floor made it easy to carry, as did tying the door open to be able to see where I was going. The total weight was about 50 pounds, and it was a breeze to move. Body heat plus a can or two of Canned Heat kept it cozy. A light, two-wheeled trailer carried it on the roads and trails to our fishing spots.

Now this may sound like a "Rube Goldberg," but it was much nicer than the arrangement Eddie Goupell and I used on the Chain Lakes 60 years ago. A sled carried our fishing gear plus two or three heavy blankets, a spud, and a hatchet. The routine was to spud exploratory holes, cut three or four two-inch poles about six feet long, place them in a teepee arrangement, and drape blankets to provide a dark interior. A small box provided the seat. Then the wait as one moved the decoy to attract the northern pike into spearing distance. It could be a long wait. We had our good times and often brought some good-sized fish home.

In another year, about 1937, I had built a big, sturdy shanty and placed it about where the Shivaree has been held off County Road 489. I invited Ralph King to join me. Before he arrived, I had made a decoy of a very large northern pike and had maneuvered it out of eye range. After watching the empty hole for some time, I carefully pulled the string and brought the big decoy into spearing range. Ralph got excited and carefully took aim. When the fish was in range, he let his spear go. "I got him!" yelled Ralph, and he retrieved the fish. But when he pulled it in, he said he had been tricked. We both had a good laugh. I don't remember if we actually got a keeper or not, but we both still remember that outing.

From the Riverbank
October 25, 1996

Rabbit Hunting with Old Gyp

Being allowed to play hooky from school to hunt with Dad put life in perspective.

October 15, 1930, dawned brightly. This was opening of small game season. Old Gyp, our dog, was ready; the shotguns were oiled and ready also. But it was midweek, and Clarence and I were in school.

When we went home for lunch, Dad said, "How would you boys like to go rabbit hunting?" Our hopes soared, but what about school?

Dad reached for the phone, ringing Central, and gave a number. "George (Wilson, our school principal was on the other end of the line), this is Oscar Roberts, and I'm going to take my boys rabbit hunting this afternoon." No asking if it was all right, just stating a fact.

We were overjoyed, and it didn't take long to change into our old clothes. As soon as we took the guns down off the gun rack, Old Gyp went nuts. My 12th birthday was the next day, and I think this was kind of a birthday gift.

Our destination was a small cedar swamp on the east side of the Rainy River, about two miles north of Four Mile Road. This being my first rabbit hunt, Dad put me on a big hollow stump, saying, "Just stay right here, and Gyp will bring a rabbit right to you."

It wasn't long until the music of a good rabbit dog perked up my "high" of actually having a shotgun at the ready, and as I looked upstream to the source of Gyp's barking, I saw a jack rabbit heading right for the stump I was standing on. Now I was really nervous. I raised the gun but then put it down, thinking the rabbit was too far away. Now it was too close. Turning around, I watched the rabbit pass me by. A shotgun barked, and a clear "I got it!" came from Clarence.

Gyp repeated this same circle with another rabbit, with the same scenario. Firing a gun at a running jack rabbit was something that wasn't going to come easy. The third trip around, I blasted almost point blank with the rabbit only five or six feet from me. I got the rabbit, but there wasn't much left of it. At least I was redeemed in Gyp's thinking, as he stopped to shake what was left of my prize. Thank goodness my Dad and Clarence had much better luck than I had.

Actually it was experience, and at subsequent outings, I began to understand what to do and when to do it. This was a day I would like to live forever—hunting with my dad and brother while other kids were cooped up in school.

From the Riverbank
November 11, 1997

Thanksgiving Headshot Rabbit

Everyone knows why shotguns are used to hunt, but here's a different approach.

Thanksgiving had some rituals at our house as I was growing up. One was for all the male members to go rabbit hunting. It was hard to round up enough artillery for the outing. There were two Remington pump 20 gauge, a 16 gauge single shot, and also a single shot .22 rifle, and we could borrow Grandpa Fairman's double-barreled 12 gauge. That left us one gun shy.

One year Dad said that he would hunt with his .38 Smith & Wesson revolver. But when we started rounding up ammunition, there were no shells for the revolver. We stopped at Everling's garage, and when Hod Bonner asked who was going to hunt rabbits with a revolver, Dad spoke up. "I'll shoot them!" Hod started laughing and rashly claimed he would eat the head of any rabbit that fell to my Dad's revolver.

The rabbits were white, not spooky at all, and you guessed it. Dad shot a rabbit right through the head. It was a riot when we all showed up at Everling's and the "head-shot" rabbit was tossed down on the counter right in front of Hod Bonner! What a lot of fun that was. This story is among the finest of my Thanksgiving recollections.

From the Riverbank
January 5, 1994

Muzzleloaders and Homemade Bullets

Boys are full of mischief as they strive to imitate men.

Muzzleloaders finished out the deer firearm season, and some hunters were successful with them. Most certainly they had the woods pretty much to themselves.

My dad bought a Civil War muzzleloading musket and a hex barrel rifle that were similar to the guns he hunted with as a teenager (around the turn of the century). His tales of muzzleloading guns sparked my interest, and I started a plan to do some pioneer shooting. Doing it "strictly on the sly," there was a lot of improvising to do.

First of all, no percussion caps were available, so a .22 short casing was filed down, making a satisfactory cover for the nipple, and the white phosphorus tips of wooden matches made an acceptable minor explosion. However, the smokeless powder used in 1930 vintage shotgun shells didn't ignite well and only made a mild "whoosh" as the charge left the barrel. Time to get really serious! Eddie Goupell filched some black powder shells from his dad's collection of old buffalo rifle shells. We carefully pried out the slugs (these were the real thing, and a false move could cause a serious explosion). When it came to loading the powder, we felt that if a little bit was okay, a lot more would be better. We swiped some lead-headed roofing nails from the elevator lumber yard. Removing the lead from the nails, we thought we had really good bullets.

When all was in readiness, we headed to the Long Swamp along the railroad grade that terminated at the limestone quarry at Black Lake near the old haunted house. We took turns carrying the dangerous weapon, hoping to see a rabbit or a squirrel. Seeing no game, we headed back, knowing that one of us had to shoot the muzzleloader. For the first time this day, we both became scared of actually shooting it. After some false starts, we decided to lay flat on the ground, putting the barrel under the ground-level bottom fence wire. But who was brave enough to touch it off?

Since Eddie was a couple of years older than me (I think I was about 13 at the time), by default it became his lucky day. Eddie aimed at a big rock about 100 feet from the fence and fired. The black powder boomed, and the nail-head bullets zinged. When the smoke cleared, we could see where some of the projectiles had hit the rock. Eddie was lucky that he was already laying flat and the barrel was securely held down by the fence wire. He complained of a sore shoulder and a slight, temporary loss of hearing. We soberly sneaked the muzzleloader back to its proper place and didn't do much bragging about it until a few weeks later. Boy, did that black powder smell good! Eddie often told his boys that we grew up in the best of times. Plenty of game to hunt, lots of fish to catch, and being able to make the most of it.

On another of our escapades along the Long Swamp grade, our dog Gyp got a rabbit started. When it came into the open where Eddie, Elmer McClellan, and I stood, a .22 rifle shot rang out, and a monstrous black and white rabbit kicked its last. We think it had gotten loose from Hart's. There would be no taking this rabbit home. After dressing it out and cooking it over an open fire, we had some tough chewing, and with no salt or pepper. But our old dog Gyp didn't mind. He ate his share and mine too.

From the Riverbank
December 28, 2000

Sledding and Skiing

Sledding was a favorite childhood activity. We fit it in whenever we could, sometimes to our own peril.

After a few puny winters with not too much snow plus mild temperatures, we are faced with a lot of early snow plus the earliest freeze-up of Black Lake for a long time. This is starting out to be a real, honest-to-goodness winter. Takes me back to when the hills on either side of the old school were real challenges for anyone with a sled during January and February.

The old school property was located between School Street on the west and College Street on the east, while Shaw Street bounded the north side. School Street was the best hill, and since the fourth, fifth, and sixth grades were in the West building, we could get at least two downhill rides during recess. By running up the road past Dr. Bruce's house, we had clear sailing until Shaw Street loomed ahead. Then was decision time, depending on how much snow or ice was on the hill.

Snow prompted us to make a right turn heading east, and this was done by dragging a right toe while turning the steering bar hard to the right. Here was where we had to watch out for horse-drawn rigs, but if all was clear, we reversed the tactic and turned left. If we were lucky, we could get all the way to Bye's or Smitty's or Edna Lound's (take your pick, depending on who owned the little store that is now occupied by Dr. Willey).

If the hill was especially icy, approaching Shaw Street caused almost panic. Two choices, and both very dangerous. Either head for the snow bank to slow down, or take a chance at steering for a narrow pathway between Doc McNeil's fence and Ma Guinther's house. If you weren't apprehended by an irate homeowner waving a sturdy broom, the next maneuver was to jump off your sled at the alley, and that was enough excitement for one recess! Boys who didn't get back into their seats on time were denied the privilege of bringing their sled to school for a few days.

My big brothers made some quite good skis with help from Dad. Two white ash boards about 3 1/2" wide and 7 feet long were planed and smoothed; they were then put into the copper clothes boiler with boiling water and heated until they would bend easily. It was then possible to bend the turned up front and secure it with haywire until the ski was fully dried and shaped. Leather straps would hold them on. When properly waxed, they made quite good skis.

The tanks hill, facing toward the west, was the one selected for skiing. The older boys got daring and found a 50-gallon barrel and built a jump-off place. There were no Olympic trials on that hill! We were lucky if we could even stand up, yet some of the more daring fellows made the jump, risking broken bones or bruises at the least.

The hills of Onaway were great places to play on. Few if any cars to watch out for and the streets were never salted or sanded. Life was very good for kids without a lot of responsibilities.

From the Riverbank
April 4, 1997

The Last Bell

Lunch at home on a school day was a treat, and it taught us about timeliness as well.

It was a sunny day in mid-April of 1927. We Roberts kids went home from school for our noon lunch. We lived in the white house adjacent to the Hankey Milling Company elevator, and it was quite a hike to get out of school at noon, run the four and a half blocks home, and get our lunch, usually a slab of good homemade bread with jelly or jam and milk. Since we had our own cow, milk was plentiful, and Mother's bread was wonderful. There wasn't much time to waste to get back to school before the last bell rang.

Sometimes there were noon chores such as emptying the washtubs on Monday or possibly filling the wood box, which should have been done before going to school. If we headed back to school by 12:45, there was no problem. But if we dawdled our time away and the first bell was already ringing as we headed south past Billy Beale's, John Leopard's, Russ Hitzert's, the bank, and Dave Tucker's place, the last bell was already tolling when we arrived. Clark Buehl always seemed to slow the cadence of the bell, as if to give a slight reprieve for the last-minute stragglers.

The school I am referring to was the big yellow building at the corner of Shaw and College Streets. If I was on time and didn't have to run, I usually went up the six steps on the north end of the building and entered the vestibule where the janitor (we had never heard the word *custodian* in those days) waited with watch in hand, ready to ring the last bell. The First Grade Room was on the left, and the Second Grade Room was across a wide hallway. The Kindergarten Room was at the end of the hallway and was a beautiful, large room that had windows on the east, south, and west. The Boy's Room was on the first floor beyond the stairway that led to the second floor.

If the last bell was ringing, I ran to the west entrance and fairly flew up the stairway to the Third Grade Room, which was above the Kindergarten Room and had windows on three sides. If we didn't get into our seats before the bell quit tolling, Nellie Barnes would write our names on the blackboard, and we would either miss our afternoon recess or have to stay after school.

The rest of the upstairs was occupied by the Presque Isle County Normal School, with one room for the Teacher Training and the other room to house the elementary children. Many young men and women attended the Normal School, and after one year of intensive studies, they were presented a two-year limited certificate, which enabled them to teach in rural schools for two years. They then had to go to summer school at one of the State Normal Colleges or take extension classes to extend their teaching certificate.

I always dreaded being late for school and learned two things from the times I was late. Plan my time better, and practice running faster!

From the Riverbank
January 23, 1998

Ice Skating in Onaway

Even skating rinks have history!

The earliest memories I have of ice skating are connected with Tuft's Pond. Just in case you don't remember the spot, think of an imaginary South Sixth Street (almost straight south across M-68 from the Doll House). This was also a good place to trap muskrats before it became a skating pond in winter.

The next skating rink that comes to mind was in two vacant lots on Main Street, just west of the Dairy Queen. Two large store buildings had burned down (don't know the year), and the perimeter foundations made an excellent place for the city to attach a fire hose to a corner hydrant and flood the area for a rink. It was just two blocks from our house. After school and evenings were shared there until we became too cold or wet.

The next skating rink was bigger, covering most of the present Maxon Field. The city did a masterful job of flooding this rink and then built a beautiful ice castle at the north end. Big blocks of ice from Tower Pond were used for the creation. It was even lighted for night skating, a family pastime. This was in the early 1940s. I still have my figure skates from this era. My brother Arden was an excellent skater, but try as I would, I just skated.

Not on the Road
March 3, 1993

Granddaddy Winters

I remember well those "real winters" of snow and ice.

As this winter appears ready to wind down, I hear lots of comments about the "real winters" of the past. Although the amounts of snow haven't been spectacular this winter, we have had some cold weather. But the winter of 1933 was a real blinger.

February overnight temperatures went down regularly to -30° and -45°F that year, while daytime highs hovered between -10° to zero. With less than average snow cover, the frost went deep. City water lines froze in the northern part of Onaway and didn't thaw until mid-April. For some reason, the water line to the barn, a part of the elevator property, didn't freeze. Families from a number of blocks regularly got their water at the barn until their water lines thawed.

Ray Young shared with me that the granddaddy of snow storms came to Onaway on February 22, 1922. The streets were blocked for a whole week. Ray worked at Lobdell Emery Rim Factory and reported that many roofs collapsed in the plant, damaging line shafts and lots of other mechanical parts. Since phone lines were down, messages were sent via D & M telegraph lines, via Morse code only, to Rogers City and then to Cleveland, Ohio. The messages then went to Morley Hardware and other suppliers in Saginaw and Bay City. It was weeks before the repair parts arrived on a special D & M freight shipment. I can't verify this, as I was four years old at the time. By comparison to 1933 and 1922, we have had a very good winter.

From the Riverbank
September 10, 1993

Wintering at the Old Lumber Camp

Survival in the Depression wasn't viewed as hardship as much as it was fun for the younger generation.

My eldest brother Earl graduated from Onaway High in 1931 in the Depression. No jobs, especially for 18-year-olds. Being an outdoors person, he thought he could spend the winter at an abandoned lumber camp southeast of Onaway. He talked my cousin Glen Roberts and his friend Les Axford from Pontiac into sharing this adventure.

The camp had a partial roof, but there was enough rough-cut lumber to patch it up so that it was reasonably weatherproof. The "pioneers" got an early start in October, and by mid-November it was a snug living space. It had an old stove that served to heat the long room but also provided an oven and cooking surface.

Dad helped the boys get the camp ready to move into, and when Christmas vacation came, my brothers Clarence and Arden and I begged to be able to spend some of our school vacation at the camp. Dad, having been raised with a lumber camp background, was agreeable for us to join the "big guys." Staples such as flour, lard, coffee, seasonings, and bacon were augmented by lots of rabbits, partridges, fish from a small lake, and just possibly a deer.

There were a variety of daily jobs to be done such as preparing breakfast (making pancakes); washing dishes; getting water from the spring; and cutting and splitting wood, and bringing it inside. But no list of who would be responsible for the various tasks was made. Michigan Rummy was the deciding factor for all jobs. The loser of the last game in the evening automatically had to light the cook stove and prepare breakfast. Another game of Rummy decided who cleaned up and washed the dishes. And so it continued throughout the day. We youngsters caught on to Rummy in a hurry and could spot any person bending the rules. It was a really relaxed way to decide who did what.

Our rabbit dog Gyp was so named because he was a gypsy as he roamed around Onaway looking for handouts from Johnston's Meat Market, Pregitzer's back door for treats plus a lot of petting, and Merritt's Restaurant for a few special treats. At the camp, Gyp earned his keep by barking up a storm as he kept the jack rabbits moving just slow enough to be good targets.

There was a small lake close by, and lots of perch as well as a few pan fish and pike added variety to our meals. The lake had frozen, leaving a perfectly clear layer of ice, and it was easy to locate the fish. A piece of tin can material cut into a spinner device worked well. A scrap of rabbit flesh worked as good as any night crawler. Actually the perch probably never had tasted night crawlers.

So Gyp was the only one that did not have to know how to play Michigan Rummy. When we had to go back home and to school, all three of us brothers went home with regrets. This part of the Depression we remember well.

From the Riverbank
August 29, 1995

Blackberry Picking

Lucky the children who have tasted wild blackberries right off the bushes!

What has 57 seeds, is red when it is green, and is black when it is ripe? If you answered "the blackberry," you are right.

I often wondered why my grandparents and parents bad-mouthed blackberries and would run them through the colander to remove most of the seeds. I thought they were just right, whether "canned" in the patch as they were picked, devoured in cobblers (or "blackberry grunts"), savored in pies, or served as sauce in the wintertime. But of course I didn't have false teeth and couldn't possibly know the terror of big blackberry seeds under poorly fitting dentures. After a mouthful of blackberries, I enjoy running my tongue around the edges of my teeth, finding a big fat seed, and cracking it with my eye teeth. Awful sounding but so very satisfying.

The good old days seemed to produce monster patches of all kinds of berries, and it was so much fun to have the berry pail fill so quickly. Blackberries don't mush down like raspberries, (no holes in the center), and when you get into the ones as big as the tip of your thumb, they quickly filled your pail. The best patches grew where the lumbering or fire had disturbed the soil; when sunshine and rain could get into the soil, growing took place.

I believe that most berry seeds are already in the soil but covered a depth that keeps them dry and protected from germinating. As new lumbering takes place, light is let in, and soil is opened up and disturbed. Rain and sunshine cause the seeds to germinate, and in two or three years, the brambles mature and start producing fruit. After several years of good crops, the grasses and underbrush grow enough to cut out most of the sunshine and moisture. The growth then stops, and the cycle repeats.

I remember some super blackberry patches that produce nothing now. In fact, it is difficult to even find scrawny brambles. But if the soil is disturbed by lumbering or road making or other things, the conditions are then ripe for growing, and the new brambles erupt as if by magic.

The time to scout for blackberry patches is in early July when the large white blossoms appear. Keep that location in mind, and check back in late August to see if the rain and sunshine have brought on a good crop.

Hiking through the woods looking for woodcock and partridge will certainly clue you as to where the heavy brambles are for next year's crop. Within the last week or ten days, I have come across very prominent paths through the best berry patches, an indication that the resident berry picker, also known as the black bear, has been at work. Wild animals have had a bonanza of a year for berries and fruits. Bruin should go to his den fat and ready for the long winter's nap.

From the Riverbank
July 25, 1995

Blueberry Picking

Only the old-timers and some very lucky younger ones whose parents showed them the place still know where to find "the patch."

Blueberries or huckleberries—what do you call them? I call them good, and I enjoy the chance to pick them whenever possible. This year seems to be an average crop in some places. It takes just the right amount of rain, hot weather, and an absence of late frosts.

I come from a family of scroungers of wild fruits. We have a picture taken about 1905 that documents the Roberts family and friends at a blueberry camp off the Old State Road at the northeast corner of Black Mountain. Mid-July was the time, the haying was done, and this annual event was looked forward to with great anticipation.

My dad grew up on the homestead on North Allis Highway, often called Four Mile Road. Their log home was on the 80 acres that now has the stand of mature Norway Pines. By the way, I helped plant these trees on this piece of land, owned by the Onaway Public Schools. The year they were planted was 1940.

Getting back to the blueberry outing, it was a long way by horse and wagons to the patch. Five or six couples plus some others loaded a couple of tents, bedding, and lots of good things to eat into the wagons and plodded along the dusty, almost non-road. It required most of an afternoon to get to the area and set up camp. Berry picking began for some of the group while the others set up the camp and prepared the evening meal. The campfire was pleasant, and much storytelling and singing occupied the evening.

Picking in earnest took place as soon as the dew was off the berries. (They don't keep well if picked wet, and these had to survive this day and the long wagon ride home late the next day.) The pails and containers of berries then were placed in the shade and where there was breeze, if possible.

The men wielded mechanical berry pickers that could pick probably a quart at a swing. It's hard to explain, but a series of finger-like scoops removed the berries from the bushes and stored them in a large container. There were handles on the pickers so that one could stand upright and pick the berries with a swinging motion. There were also hand-scoop pickers as well. Naturally, a lot of leaves as well as green and overripe berries were harvested. But the berries could be picked over back at home. Winnowing also helped remove the leaves and lightweight debris.

Berry picking was always almost like an annual fun festival. No cows to milk, kids stayed home with older daughters or grandparents, and I'm sure a violin or two was tucked into the wagons. And the results were blueberry pies and quarts and quarts of berries canned for next fall and winter.

The tradition remains but in a diminished form. It takes but a few minutes to drive to the patch. No mechanical pickers are now legal (and with good reason). Not so many berries are canned these days, but pies and cobblers are still made, and some go into the freezers. We could get by without blueberries, but what fun to look forward to searching for and picking them.

From the Riverbank
October 20, 1993

Rhubarb Cellars

Here is the story of an unusual industry that sprang up during the years of the Depression.

"Pie plant," or rhubarb, was a tasty spring treat. Rhubarb pies, cobblers, and sauce let you know that summer was on the way. Then in 1933 some pioneers from Armada, in Macomb County, showed folks a new twist. Growing and picking rhubarb in December and January? And in dark cellars? This really was something new!

The MacGregors and McFalls, all members of one clan, left Armada and moved to Onaway because it was colder. They grew rhubarb, and at the end of the second year in the fields, it was plowed up in late September or early October, leaving the exposed roots to freeze. Here's where colder Onaway was the bonus. The hard freeze here was about two weeks earlier than down state, and they got at least a two-week head start in marketing the rhubarb.

After the hard freeze, they brought in the roots on stone bolts, and they were placed in open 30-foot x 100-foot cellars. The cellars were about four feet deep and could handle about an acre of frozen rhubarb roots. A center ridge pole, supported by cedar posts, was covered with boards and insulated with straw and earth. The goal was to get this part of the job done by deer season. Then, two or three wood or coal stoves were constantly fired and the roots liberally watered so that a temperature of 90 degrees could be maintained.

Most cellars were lighted with kerosene lanterns, but Gilbert MacGregor said they were lucky to have electric lights. The rhubarb grew rapidly once the cellar and roots were warmed up. This beautiful crop grew three or four inches a day. It was packed in light green boxes, about 15 inches long and 4 x 5 inches wide, and five pounds of rhubarb just filled them. Strawberry and Victoria varieties produced bright stems and a very small, yellowish-green leaf. They were classified as choice, fancy, and select. The cases were delivered to the Railway Express office at the D & M depot in Onaway, and several tons per day were shipped to markets in Chicago, New York City, Philadelphia, Pittsburgh, and other northern markets. More southerly cities were supplied by outside growers from Florida.

The price varied according to supply and demand and if the rhubarb arrived in good condition. Kenny McFall said they tried different wholesalers, always looking for a better price. The harvesting, started by Christmas, continued for about six weeks.

It was an absolutely beautiful sight to walk into the cellars, wait for your eyes to adjust to the low-light level, and see this crop of bright red and green being harvested and packed for shipment. It was hard work, and the women of the families often did the grading and packing. It was a good cash crop, and at a time of the year when everything else was "down." And remember, this was at the bottom of the Depression, so anything to make money was tried.

The Andrew Scott family, related to the MacGregors and McFalls, moved up two or three years later and got into rhubarb growing in heated cellars. Others who raised rhubarb were Beecher Warren, Walt Van Zant, Charley Minser, Henry Schmidt, Peter Russell, George Baker, and probably many others as well. The competition was keen, and then the Railway Express got higher. Finally sometime about 1945, Railway Express discontinued the rail service and pretty well put an end to an era of rhubarb cellars around Onaway. You can still see some stone walls that were a part of the rhubarb cellars. When you see rhubarb growing in unaccountable places, it's just possible that it is part of the past. It was a special time in Onaway's development.

From the Riverbank
September 14, 2000

Old-Time Jelly Making

Making jelly is a labor of love.

Outdoor living, camping, and picking wild fruits and berries have always been a part of the Roberts family heritage and practice. The purchase of a book several years ago has given additional dimensions to our scrounging for foods. *Stalking the Wild Asparagus*, by Euell Gibbons, is a fascinating invitation to experience some of the old-time ways and have a lot of fun doing it.

One recipe for old-time blackberry jelly called for gathering blackberries and wild apples. We took no shortcuts such as Sure Jell or commercial pectin, but meticulously followed Euell Gibbons' instructions. We quickly discovered that it was lots of work and time-consuming. To the best of our recollections, it was just the way we remembered our mothers had made jelly. Jelly bags hanging and dripping and the wonderful aromas and stains on so many things, including hands, were reminiscent of childhood days.

I can now better appreciate the jams and jellies I had as a youngster, and I still remember how I hated to empty the pulp from the jelly bag. Our chickens came running to enjoy the seeds and apple bits, helping to make jelly making a completely 'waste not' operation.

As we select the jams and jellies from stores, and they are good, I can recall with real pleasure the fun and processing of the ingredients. While this is not a book review, I can enthusiastically endorse the back-to-nature hominess that comes out clearly in *Stalking the Wild Asparagus* by Euell Gibbons.

From the Riverbank
December 22, 2000

Bread Baking

Boys built brawn by cranking the bread blender.

It took a lot of food to fill up our family. My parents and seven children put nine of us around the table three times a day. Bread was a staple, and it required nine loaves of homemade bread each seven days. I don't know how many bread tins our oven could hold at one time; I don't think nine, so bread-making day was a big event.

Somewhere along in my young years, my dad bought a bread mixer. It was a large, tinned, bucket-like thing that could be fastened to the top of a kitchen stool by a clamp that kept it secure. After all the ingredients were put into the bread mixer, a triangular cover with a long, curved mixing arm was clamped to the top. Then the work began, and this is where strong-armed boys could be conscripted to turn the crank and mix the dough.

Mother was the inspector, and when we thought we had turned the crank enough, we asked for an opinion. Usually we were just getting tired and wished to be relieved, and Mom would say, "Just another ten minutes." Eventually the bread would sit for a while after being punched down, and then the turning process started all over. If we were able to sneak off so some of the other brothers could be pressed into "slave labor," we would stay out of sight.

The bread was then cut into the right size loaves to fill the bread tins. When it raised this time, it was popped into the old wood-fired kitchen range. If all went well, and after being checked by Mom, out came the golden crusted bread. There were times that a too hot oven produced some scorched loaves.

The elevator was close enough to our house that the great aroma of fresh bread would reach Dad's nostrils, and he'd come to investigate. He would find just the best loaf, as it was on the cooling rack, take out his pocket knife, and slit it from end to end, peeling out the soft center and spreading the crust parts with fresh butter and jam. Then he would beat a retreat to the office in the elevator. Mom would be upset. What to do with the soft center of the bread? But in a way, I sometimes think she was pleased that her husband enjoyed her baking so well that he wanted to enjoy it at its very best.

    I hated it when it was my turn to wash supper dishes on bread-baking days. All the bread tins and also the job of washing that monster of a bread mixer. But the homemade bread was so great that the chores involved in turning the mixer, washing the tins, etc., were worth it. And with a number of boys around, just by chance we only had to help once or possibly twice a week.

From the Lakeshore
August 1, 2003

The Onaway Fairgrounds

Our local fair was a Disneyland for us kids.

Memories from the Onaway Fairgrounds go back at least 75 years, and what a glorious place it was for a nine-year-old kid. Very little remains to even suggest that there was such place, but recently I took a picture that brought back clear recollections that I will share with you.

Located just one mile north of State Street on M-95 (M-211) stood this wonderland. It was enclosed by 8' or 10' ship-lapped boards brilliantly painted with advertisements by most major stores and commercial enterprises. It was a sight to behold. Behind the fence were more shops, display areas, and a midway for the usual circus-like shows. "Barkers" shouted their wares, strong man games, slot machines. Winnings were tokens that could be traded for candy or soft drinks and were accepted by most shops for rides.

Frank Gregg, grandson of Will and Mae Gregg, was visiting with his relatives. Since we were the same age, we chummed up and visited the Fair together. After looking over most of the stalls and games, we were fascinated by the "one-armed bandit" (slot machine). We didn't have many nickels, but we got on a lucky streak and had a pocketful of tokens that we could have cashed in for real money. But no. Suckers that we were, we fed the bandit until our pockets were empty. I learned a good lesson that day, and my urge for gambling was whetted and lost all in one short afternoon!

On to the big spectacular for the day. A bi-plane and a red convertible were to race ten laps around the half-mile track. The plane had difficulty making the tight turns, and the car had to have two fellows stand on the running boards to keep it from skidding and possibly turning over. What a thrilling race for third graders to watch, and of course we had to get as close to the action as possible and get chased back away from the railings. I don't know if there was a winner, but it was a good show.

At the quarter mile race track, horses pulled sulky carts (bicycle-like tires and shafts with the horses between), and drivers talked to and sometimes used the whips to urge on their horses. There was a judging stand where old Jim Snody plus some elderly horse enthusiasts rang the starting bell, called the racers back on false starts, and waved the flag for the winner and second and third places. Fred Clemens was a race horse owner who used to exercise his horses one at a time by driving his car and holding the bridle of the horse through the open window. He knew exactly how fast the horse was going.

The well was on the very south end of the fairgrounds just inside the fence. There was a hole under the fence that an energetic nine-year-old could climb through and avoid the entrance fee, which was probably not more than a dime for small kids, but the thrill of getting in free made the effort worthwhile.

From the Riverbank
July 20, 1994

The County Fair of 1928

My friend Roy showed me how heroes were made.

As I drove past the old county fair site last week, I was reminded of the County Fair of 1928. A hot-air balloon was being readied for a stunt man to parachute from. The day was cold, the balloon didn't inflate well, and it didn't get high enough. When the parachutist jumped, it was the trees east of M-95 that saved him from injury. Roy Brown took off running, following the path of the empty balloon.

The next day, the sheriff, the owner of the balloon, and the stunt man showed up at our fourth grade classroom door. We thought Roy was in trouble when they asked him to step out into the hallway. He told them he could take them exactly to where the balloon went down.

So Roy became my hero. He got off school half a day and got a like-new five dollar bill to boot. This is how heroes are made.

From the Riverbank
June 24, 2001

Boy Scout Bugling

My start in music came through the Boy Scouts. Learning to play the bugle well came out of some early badgering.

Boy Scouts was mostly a family tradition. I became a Tenderfoot in 1931, following in the footsteps of my brothers Homer (who also was Assistant Scoutmaster for Superintendent Glen Schoenhals) and Clarence. Arden also followed in scouting. Homer brought home a bugle, and we all had fun learning all the calls. We took our turns standing on the porch and blowing it.

I recall one early morning when Pat Young stopped by and asked me, "How much do you get paid for making such awful noise as you practice?"

Naturally I was surprised, thinking he was going to compliment me for such a display of colorful martial music. I was abashed, not knowing what to say. "I am pleased to play the bugle," I replied.

He cut me off and said, "Kid, I'll pay you fifty cents a week if you quit blowing into that miserable thing!"

But being a bugler offered many fun experiences. Fourth of July parades were more fun if you were in the Drum & Bugle Corps and marched the length of Onaway streets. A special treat was to go to the Veterans CCC camp at Clear Lake to play retreat when Old Glory was lowered from the flagpole. There were other perks. We got to eat in the Officer's Mess Hall. We learned that better food was served there and lots of it. Mr. Lewellyn Karr often would provide transportation. Mr. Karr was a biology teacher as well as one of my Sunday school teachers. He always supported scouting in many ways.

Having been in the Drum & Bugle Corps was a perfect stepping stone to play in The Onaway Volunteer Band in the early to mid-1930s. Also a stint in the Rogers City Band and later in the college marching and concert bands. So I'm glad I didn't take the fifty cents a week from Pat Young and stop playing the bugle.

From the Riverbank
Date Unknown

The Onaway City Band

Playing in the city band was a big deal for me and so many of my friends.

I got to thinking of the Onaway City Band in the early 1930s and how it got started. Cheboygan City Band had gone defunct, and the city offered the sale of the band instruments if some group would buy all of them. Merl Smith, Herb Leffler, and some other Onaway musicians canvassed the town, trying to find enough people who were interested in forming a band and able to help pay for the instruments. A deal was struck, and the Onaway City Band was organized in late 1931 or early 1932. Director Merl Smith, Business Manager Herb Leffler, and musicians and would-be musicians gathered in the large upstairs room of the City Hall (current museum) to organize and practice every Thursday night. What a smoke-filled den that was. We non-smokers came home smelling horrible! I don't know if music runs in families, but as I list the make-up of the band, you might think so.

Merl Smith was our director and an outstanding coronet player who had been a member of the John Phillip Sousa Band while still a late teenager. (When Merl Smith moved to Saginaw, Carl became our director.) Other trumpet or coronet players included Bob Smith, Eddie Goupell, Marvel Leffler, and Bud Stout. Clarinet players were Roland Koepsel, Homer Roberts, and Harry Bye. Harry was a real virtuoso from earlier times and played only part of the time. The saxophone section was composed of Mike Merritt, C-melody; Doll Noon, B flat soprano; and Carl McClutchey, E flat alto. We had a big trombone section headed by Herb Leffler, Jack Lee, and Eddie Kapalla. I played a valve trombone and then switched to a baritone to help Ed Smith in the baritone section. The mellophones were played by Arnold Leffler and Bud McCormick. Earl McCormick played the bass drum, and Clarence Roberts played snare drums. The bass horns were played by Frank Smith, Maitland McCormick, and Frank Welch.

Much of our music came with the instrument deal from the City of Cheboygan. We practiced endlessly at home, and the Thursday night practice put new music in front of us. The make-up of the band changed a little in the mid-thirties after the Onaway School Band was organized. We played weekly concerts in the summer on the approximate location of the Chamber of Commerce information booth. Folding chairs were brought in, but most of the audience sat in their cars. Applause was car horns blowing. How sweet that music!

From the Riverbank
December 15, 1993

Blacktopping

There's no dust from a blacktopped road, particularly when you help build it.

The trip from Onaway to Atlanta in 1936 was gravel and dust all the way. Whether it was Montmorency County politics or what, blacktopping from the Presque Isle to the Montmorency County line to Atlanta was done in 1937. Onaway was the rail head where road tar could be delivered, and a siding behind the elevator was selected to "spot" the tank cars carrying the semi-liquid asphalt.

I had just graduated from Onaway High School and was lucky to get the job of steaming the tank cars to a temperature high enough for the tar to be pumped into truck tankers. The construction company brought in a 20-horsepower vertical boiler as the source of steam. I connected the steam output of the boiler to a pipe put in the tank car. A series of pipes ran back and forth in the car, and when enough steam passed through them, the tar would be warmed enough to be pumped out.

It took anywhere from eight to ten hours to heat the tank. I'd call Ed Smozzle, and he would send in trucks to deliver the hot tar to the "batch plant" just east of Clear Lake. If it rained or the weather turned cold, it took another four or five hours to bring up the temperature.

Sadly enough, I was paid by the car, not for the hours I put in. I built a small protected area to shield myself the sun and rain and had a rocking chair to relax. Every few hours I checked the water level in the gauges, and if the water in the boiler was low, I manually opened valves to inject water into the boiler.

One extra dreary night, I awakened at 3 a.m. to see no water in the gauge! Only two things possible: inject water into the possibly dry boiler and blow both myself and the boiler to kingdom come, or put the fire out and run. I'm a coward, so I quickly raked the burning coal from the boiler and beat a hasty retreat. After that, I kept an alarm clock that alerted me every hour and a half.

I don't know exactly when the stretch from Onaway to the Montmorency County line was completed, but I always appreciated that first stretch of blacktop and always drove to Atlanta when going from Onaway to Alpena.

From the Riverbank
February 9, 2001

The Old Library

Well-worn steps testify to the draw of the Old Library.

Have you taken the opportunity to visit the now completed library in the lower level of the courthouse? It is just great and so pleasant to browse through.

This brings me back to the library that was part of the old high school. As you walked up the sidewalk then the three or four steps, you were on the landing, ready to open the doors to enter the building. The last time I walked up those steps, they were so worn by thousands and thousands of feet that they were dish shaped! From the inside landing, you walked up the first flight of steps, made a left turn, continued past the principal's office, and there you were at the library.

The room was divided so that the charge out desk was on the left and there was a tall desk barrier preventing one from getting into the stacks of books. Mrs. David Yeager, the librarian, would help you find books and invite you behind the barrier to get information from the specialized books too large to take to the library tables.

There were tables and chairs capable of seating about 40 persons. I recall that the student council regularly met there as well as other clubs. This part of the library also was used by community groups for special meetings.

Mrs. Yeager selected students to assist younger classes. We didn't have much in the way of books at home, and I checked out lots of books. I remember being called the "the bookworm" at home, trying to avoid chores, etc., by claiming the need to read for reports. Sometimes it worked, but not always.

I'm not sure if the library also was used as a public library, but it sure was one of my favorite places. Mrs. Yeager lived on my street, and her grandson Perry Yeager was one of my best friends until he moved to Mackinaw City after the Big Fire of 1926.

* * *

Yes, I got a bit of ribbing about smelling spring last week, yet there were a number of folks who confirmed that on a special day they actually had the feeling that spring was on the way.

Last Sunday another sign of spring reached my ears. It was the sweet sound of the chickadee changing to the "fee-bee" song. Those of us lucky enough to have lots of chickadees in our yards keep listening for that cheery song. Spring can't be too far behind.

From the Riverbank
May 22, 1998

Decoration Day Visits to Gravesites

Memorial Day weekend has become a national holiday, used by most as a time for travel or recreation. Here is a look at what the day used to entail.

Decoration Day was something we could always count on. May 30 was the day our family set aside to go to the North Allis Cemetery to spruce up the gravesites of our ancestors. This was a very solemn occasion, and families came a few weeks or days ahead of time to grub out the weeds, remove old flower pots, and bring new geraniums and other hardy flowers.

Helping water plants was a joy for us small boys. The pump never kept its prime, and we always brought a jug of water from home in case someone forgot to leave some water in the bucket beside the pump. Pouring water down the top of the pump and then pumping like crazy was what it took to get a few buckets of water to carry to the various gravesites. After tending the Fairman plots (Mother's family), we pitched in and worked on the Roberts family sites.

Small children took pride in how the cemetery looked as we completed our work. Then came the leisurely walk around the entire cemetery as our parents reintroduced us to the various pioneer names and possibly some anecdotes that helped us connect ourselves and family with the very old Onaway history. If we were lucky, we would startle a cottontail rabbit from her nest of babies and get a chance to admire how cute they were. A very special treat was when the American Legion Color Guard would arrive, take down all the old flagsticks from the graves of veterans, and put up new flags. We hoped they would give us some of the old flagsticks. Then the solemn moments when the Color Guard would stand at attention, bring their rifles up, and fire a salvo. We always wondered if they were blank, but we scrambled to pick up the empty shells.

Then it was time to go home and plant the family garden. This, too, was a Decoration Day ritual. The garden had been plowed and harrowed, but it took a lot of raking to remove the top stones to get it ready for seeding. There was a job for all of us. After the rows had been marked off and opened for seeds, the younger among us could drop the big seeds such as beans, corn, squash, etc., while skilled hands planted the finer seeds. Since our garden was right next to the elevator, and Dad sold seeds and fertilizer, we used lots of both. He wanted to have customers see how well seeds from Hankey Milling Co. grew! I don't know if we got the garden completely planted on Decoration Day, but I remember it was a hard work day.

But now it is Memorial Day, and it is celebrated so that a three-day holiday is possible. We all celebrate it in our many different ways. We whose loved ones have chosen cremation may not have that special place to cut the grass, place the flowers, etc. I will still visit the North Allis Cemetery.

PART TWO

Life On The Riverbank

The serenity of the bank of the Black River framed many observations on family, nature, and life. The riverbank provided a sense of place and meaning. The stories that follow show the depth of life, not only for me but others. It was a wonderful home from 1977 to 2002.

The riverbank was also a place from which to look forward. The fishing was great, neighbors good, but I always had a yearning to live where we could enjoy glorious sunrises, sunsets, and moonscapes that living in the woods did not provide. When I sold Riverhouse and moved to the west side of Black Lake, all of these special things were added. But sandy soil could not provide the very good gardening possibilities of the riverbank location. We win some, and we lose some.

From the Riverbank
September 1, 2000

Watching Birds Fish

The Riverhouse on Cope Rd. was home for 25 years, from 1977-2002. Situated on the banks of the Black River, it was a great place for watching wildlife. Bird watching was especially delightful.

Across from Riverhouse is a quite deep hole in the Black River that tapers off into shallow water, a fringe of reeds, and finally into swamp-like woods. As we are seated at the dining table or enjoying the screened porch, we observe a lot of wildlife activities over there.

The fishing hole attracts a variety of birds that like to fish, and many strategies are employed to "fill their creel." Early spring is the season for mergansers (American hooded and red-breasted), and they all dive and then swim under the water to catch their meals. As soon as the surrounding lakes are free of ice, the mergansers shift their fishing grounds to the lakes.

The banded kingfishers stake out their territory and leisurely fish as they dig out and refurbish their long nest hole near the top of a clay or sand bank along the river. They then lay their eggs and pick up the tempo of their fishing as their babies start crying for food. A snag of tree just above the fishing hole is a lookout station, and their keen eyesight lets them see minnows and small fish. Their method is to dive straight into the water and spear the food with their sharp bill. They go from one fishing spot to another, making their presence known by their chattering voice. Young birds come with their parents, watch just how to do it, and eventually, by trial and error, finally master the art of spearing minnows.

I recently heard a friend wishing for the patience of a great blue heron. In recent weeks, we have been fortunate to see this patience being practiced. Out of the reeds and thick grass across and downstream, a heron stealthily moves upstream. A long stop to survey every inch of its surrounding, then turning slowly to pick a red berry, it continues as it steps into knee-deep water and comes to a total statue-like stop.

Only the eyes now move as it judges the distance to the minnow or frog, and then with a swift jab of the neck, the hapless food item becomes part of a meal. The slow upstream movement continues, the heron stepping over some tree limbs, moving into the fringe of the swamp, and back to another likely fishing stand.

Now I begin to appreciate the patience of the great blue. An hour or two may be required to fill the gullet, and if it has a nest of young in a heron rookery, this process must be repeated many times during the day. The nest may be several miles from each fishing spot, and the lone heron in flight is probably on one of many forays to bring food back to the rookery. It regurgitates the food for the hungry brood and then goes back to another food gathering mission.

All of the birds have special ways of capturing food and training their offspring to learn to capture their own. Although they all dip into the same pool, their methods are so different, yet the pool continues to feed them all.

* * *

A lone American merganser dives for minnows across the river. Probably one of a clutch of eight or ten that we frequently saw during the summer. Too many raccoons along this river and they kill at least half the young waterfowl. Yet next spring at least a pair of each kind will show up and the cycle will be repeated. The mood of the river is somber, and the very last of the fallen leaves that so recently graced the flowing water have been carried downstream and are now at the stream bottom, making the special compost nutrient of all rivers. It truly must be fall.

From the Riverbank
Date Unknown

Wildlife on the River

The screened porch at Riverhouse offered great viewing of wildlife on both sides of the river.

Scanning logs across the river at breakfast time presents a variety of animal life. Spring sunshine brings out the turtles and later the mallards. As soon as the drake only shows up, I can be sure the hen is incubating her eggs back away from the water. Later the wood ducks come, and young mallards follow parent birds as they search for bugs and other food.

But now the merganser crop from the spring hatch are showing up and sunning themselves right where the parent birds rested in springtime. Late afternoon is the time when jays, robins, and doves seek the protection of the logs and bathe. Northern pike also seek the shadow of the logs, and woe be to the small birds that are active when the pike is present. Once in a rare while, a great blue heron checks in to do a little fishing.

* * *

Wildlife along the riverbank is a changing show, and currently the dominant actors are a small flock of partridges. They generally come from the same direction and stop in the thick brush to check the open space, which is our view of the river. If the coast is clear, they slowly step out into the opening and head for cover. If a motion is detected from our windows, they start to race for the opposite side and may end up bursting into noisy flight. This routine is repeated until all five or six birds reach their favorite feeding place. Then, one by one, they fly across the river to prepare for their night plans, probably hunkering in a cedar or balsam tree. At least one of them today is a male, and he is already strutting his stuff, just like a Tom Turkey.

From the Riverbank
April 25, 1997

Otters on the Riverbank

While we lived on Black River and enjoyed its activities, it was our tradition to keep track of the happenings at Black Lake as well, especially the annual "ice out" event.

The Riverbank has been teeming with activity this past week. The "fun guys" of the river showed up Sunday morning and put on a real clown act for us. Otters are such neat animals! Mink are quite regular visitors, but since the snow has melted, it is very difficult to notice them. (While Florence was proofreading this column, two mink loped across our yard just outside our front door, and a third was seen on the opposite side of the river.) Mergansers continue to charm us as well as the "woodies" and mallards. I have advice for our turkeys: Don't trust anyone!

Another activity on the riverbank is trimming weeds and raking leaves, especially on the steeply sloped bank. After I watched Florence almost slip towards the very cold and fast running Black River, I went to the garage and returned with a life jacket and a 30-foot piece of stout rope. "What is that for?" she asked. I tied one end of the rope to the life jacket and the other end to a large birch tree. Then Florence got the drift of what was next. She willingly donned the jacket, and she was literally tied to her work! One doesn't often get such a good and willing worker, and I didn't wish to take any chances of seeing her set off down Black River without finishing her job! To document this 'tethered bride," I took time out to snap a few pictures.

* * *

The Roberts family always kept track of Black Lake's ice out time since my grandparents first homesteaded close to the lake in the late 1870s. We tended to predict April 19 as the possible breakup date.

Could it have had anything to do with my brother Homer's birth date, April 19? Florence also has kept a log of ice out dates since 1965, and they range from April 2 in 1973 to the latest date of May 5 in 1972. However, the average dates Florence recorded were from April 14 to April 22. The earliest freeze up date Florence had recorded was December 1, 1989; the latest was January 20, 1975.

All of these dates are of interest and may help us understand why some springs seem so very long in coming. A college professor from somewhere in New York State places a call to Florence each spring for dates of the ice out. I will go out on a limb and predict ice out on Black Lake at the time you read this copy of "From the Riverbank."

* * *

A dear old friend visited me over the weekend, and I can safely say old, because Puppet is nearing seventeen years of age. Puppet is a dog that looks so very much like Wishbone on the PBS late afternoon TV. It is a long story, but Puppet once belonged to Paula (Lamberson) Chapman, and somewhere along the years, Puppet also belonged to me. During the years of our "On the Road" wanderings, I gave Puppet back to Paula, and so Puppet has been my next door neighbor for many years, residing with Marcella and Lawrence Lamberson.

Puppet visits me daily, but time takes its toll on dogs as well. Puppet no longer hears, but she still has excellent eyesight. I think Puppet is approaching the need for an "extended care facility." Still, I look forward to visits with my dear old friend.

From the Riverbank
May 9, 1997

Friendly Folk

Stopping to talk to folks is a joy, sometimes a red-faced joy.

After last week's "tethered bride" story, my friend Bob Wilton, who lives just a bit down river from Florence and me, made this observation: "I would gladly have rescued Florence had she fallen into the river. Good lawn and leaf rakers are hard to come by, and I could have used some extra help." You are all heart, Bob!

* * *

While on my way to Forest Township dump last Saturday, I noticed quite a lot of cars at Clarissa Fitzpatrick's house. I thought there must be a garage sale and I should stop there on my way home. I parked on Black River Road and walked into the garage, not even noticing that there wasn't the usual clutter one should expect at a garage sale. The door was open, and I invited myself in to inquire where the sale items were, only to be greeted by a wave of laughter from a lot of lovely ladies all dressed up for a baby shower!

My face turned red, and I was told that my eyes opened very wide and my embarrassment clearly showed. Clarissa set me at ease by assuring me that when she had a garage sale, there would be adequate signs posted and that she would let me know about it.

* * *

I always enjoy getting out to dip a few smelt each spring, and the emphasis is on few. But this spring it happened in a very different way. Florence and I were on our way to Cedarville in the Upper Peninsula to help fulfill a last wish of the late Helen Waggott. She had requested that her cremated remains be taken to the Cedar Cemetery near Cedarville.

We found the grave site of her brother, Robert Faust, and completed her wishes. On our return trip, we notice two couples who appeared to be dipping for smelt in broad daylight, and right beside Highway 134. We stopped to watch and visit, and we were pleasantly surprised to find that we were talking to a niece of R. Buregard. We shared some Onaway and family things, and then they asked if we would like some smelt. Gladly accepting enough smelt for a good meal, we scooped up snow from the roadside to fill a plastic bag, inserted the still wiggling smelt, and then put the bag into another bag of snow. We thanked them for the kindness and enjoyed fresh smelt for supper.

From the Riverbank
June 21, 1995

River Turtles

The chance to observe and record wildlife is a valued pastime.

My morning walk sometimes follows an old two-track along the river. This morning the sand was literally covered by tracks of turtles searching for places to dig holes to deposit eggs. These are what I call river turtles. They are thinner than the bells painted, and the carapace (top shell) is quite dull. They dig their nest hole with their hind legs, and after depositing the eggs, they cover them with their hind legs. The sand here is very hard and difficult to dig into. Small exploratory holes are frequent, but few are deep enough to lay eggs into. And when the turtles do find suitable soil to dig holes and deposit their eggs, the skunks, raccoons, fox, and opossum are quick to dig them up and have a meal.

A number of years ago, I observed a big snapping turtle in the process of laying eggs next to a well-traveled road. "Bob, would you mind spending the next hour watching this turtle?" My friend quickly agreed, and the watch began. The hole, about three inches in diameter and about six inches deep, was nearing completion. (This was a huge snapper, weighing about 15 pounds!) We watched and counted as the eggs were deposited into the hole. The turtle was oblivious of us, and I took many photographs at extremely close range.

When the last of the 40 eggs were laid and the covering of the eggs started, Bob and I decided that the nest was too close to the road. We would remove the eggs and bury them in a safer place. But we had a problem. Both of us were fishermen, and it almost seemed sacrilegious to be saving snapping turtles. As I picked up the turtle and put it in a grassy ditch some distance from the road, its hind legs continued to move in the hole-covering motions. I suspect it moved the legs the exact number of times that were required to dig the hole. We moved the eggs to what I thought was a great place, dug a hole, and re-planted all 40 eggs. I checked the spot about a month later, and the nest had been dug up by a fox or some other wild animal. I have a very good set of colored slides documenting the whole show.

* * *

The yellow-bellied sapsucker is a beautiful bird, but sometimes it is a real nuisance. They are the birds that drum on most anything metal during the courtship period. Their manner of getting food also can bug you. They drill a series of horizontal holes in the bark of many trees and come back to suck the sweet sap that runs from the puncture of the cambium layer. Birches, wild cherries, and especially mountain ash trees are high on their list of trees to tend. They fly from tree to tree, sucking sap and also collecting small insects that gather to enjoy the sap. Hummingbirds especially need the small bugs to get some protein into their systems. The problem is that the mountain ash trees are often killed in this process, especially if they are small ones.

My smallish mountain ash tree will probably die within a year or two. The bird is beautiful, but it has so many bad manners, and I planted the tree in a place that it did not belong. I've decided to let nature take its course and enjoy the beauty of the bird, even if it destroys the tree.

From the Riverbank
July 3, 1998

Canoeing on the Black River

A favorite activity of our family for so many years has been canoeing, and we have come to expect the unexpected on every trip.

Kids and canoes go together, and when grandchildren visit, they are always anxious to canoe. Usually I transport kids and canoe(s) upstream, letting current return them to our front porch. Sometimes they float from out front to Tower, and Grandpa is there to return them.

Last week I was too busy to do the canoe livery thing, so the rules changed. "You can paddle upstream as far as you wish, but be sure you stop at Riverhouse on your downstream float." I didn't have much to worry about, as Katie and Lauren didn't even make it upstream past the bridge over Black River Road. I also knew that Eric and Trevor would tire before they got to Horseshoe Bend. Everything went well.

Last Saturday was time for the old folks to enjoy a float. Jockeying canoe and vehicles was a big part of the activity. I dropped off our canoe at Erratt Bridge, and then Florence followed me with the car to Tower, the where truck and trailer were parked. Getting kind of complicated? Back to where the canoe was left, and then the start of a nice float.

Nice water and mostly just steering until a very large tree blocked the total stream. It was touch and go, but we finally wiggled through. Next excitement was seeing a great-horned owl cross downstream, and then a flock of crows started harassing the owl. What a ruckus! Shortly afterwards we saw an eagle at quite close range. Chatted briefly with Ruth McFall as we floated past her river home. Later, a doe and two fawns startled us as they jumped from a small grassy island and got into the woods before the camera was reached.

We stopped just long enough at Riverhouse for clippers and a bow-saw to help clear debris left at flood time. The water slowed noticeably, and soon we saw our parked truck at Tower. Back to Erratt Bridge to get our car left there. I know it sounds complicated, but it sure is a lot of fun. We will have some aching muscles, but it was worth it all.

* * *

Did some blueberry scouting Sunday, and there will be good picking in some areas. Walking from the car, I startled a song sparrow from its nest, which revealed four or five recently hatched babies. I picked three thimblefuls of berries while Florence got enough for blueberry pancakes.

A poor choice of plains roads got the car stuck in the sand. After broken branches, etc., failed to resolve the problem, I hailed vacationers driving on M-33. Their kindness and a chain helped us out of our predicament. How great that people still help people!

From the Riverbank
Date Unknown

Log Jams and Portages

Life's journey is full of temporary setbacks and difficulties we must surmount.

Some years back, Idamae and I canoed in Ontario's wild rivers with one or two other couples. We were the senior citizens of the group. I'd like to share the story of log jams and portages and how events in life might be similar.

Log jams can be very maddening. A single log, or even a few logs, can sometimes be crossed by paddling as fast as you can (ram-speed approach). If the log is floating, it sometimes can be depressed enough to slide over. The really solid ones require you to get out onto the log, one person on either side of the canoe, and pull the canoe over the log. With 300 pounds of gear, this can be a tough pull. This step may have to be repeated several times in one jam. If enough logs are floating, they may sometimes be arranged to permit the canoe through. The solid log that sinks as you step on it can be a help or a problem. Controlled sinking can get you through, but the unexpected sinking log can get you very wet! Of course, the really big jams defy any of the above approaches, and you must resort to portaging.

So, portages are what you do when you can't do anything else! Rapids can sometimes be run, lined downed with ropes up to 100 feet long (anything you can do to make it unnecessary to unload your heavy gear), or sometimes walked through if the water isn't too deep or current too strong. But when it comes to bad rapids or falls, only the portage will do.

Portages can be welcome breaks from stretches of monotonous paddling. Portages are the common denominators in that we all participate equally in this part of the back country canoeing. Most often it is very obvious that the portage is necessary: the huge piles of logs, bad rapids, or wild falls warn us of an eminent portage. Also blazes on trees, a patch of colored cloth, a narrative on your map that says, "After you pass a large, flat rock on the …", or other directions. All out of the canoe, untie gear from the canoe thwarts, and pile it neatly at the head of the portage. While one partner balances the empty canoe's yoke on his shoulders and takes off down the "excuse" for a trail, the other partner dons a backpack and whatever else can be carried and follows the leader. It usually requires two or three round trips to complete the process.

Portages allow you to (1) regroup (sometimes canoes get separated); (2) take a "gorp" (good old raisins and peanuts) or trail food break; (3) adjust your posture; (4) take a stroll in the woods with a roll of t.p. in hand; and (5) just relax. Too often the portage is hurriedly done, but I think it is mostly where too many canoes arrive at the portage at the same time. All are concerned about jamming up the often small loading spot, and hence, a quicker removal of gear lets your canoeing friends get going sooner.

Portages let you start out fresh again, with no water in your canoe and all gear neatly stowed. I like to think these river portages are somewhat like our personal "log jams, rapids, and falls." Portages serve very useful purposes and should not be considered inevitable drudgery and work. Some of life's very best times are the portages.

From the Riverbank
July 3, 1999

Refuge at Riverhouse

Canoers were a common sight at Riverhouse, and whenever possible, our family "put in" for a float trip.

Canoeing has always been a part of our lifestyle, and living on Black River has given us opportunities to help others enjoy the fun. Groups from Lake Louise, a United Methodist Youth camp in the Wolverine area, have traditionally stopped at Riverhouse to refill their water containers, take a break, and phone the camp to report on their progress.

Several years ago, a group of ten or twelve teenage boys and two pastors made the usual stop and informed us that they would be camping at Cope Hole overnight. A monstrous thunderstorm moved in about dusk, and we were concerned about the ability of their tents to withstand the flood.

I drove to their camping location and convinced them to join us and some dry space. It wasn't too hard to sell the idea, and two trips with the pickup filled with sleeping bags and other essentials brought them to our garage. We have a large, open space upstairs in the garage, and it didn't take long for the floor area to become wall-to-wall sleeping bags. Some freshly baked brownies hit the spot, and they were snug from the night-long deluge. It was such a fun time for them, and we enjoyed being able to help.

From the Riverbank
July 20, 1994

Floating the Salmon River

A Fourth of July float trip on the Middle Fork of the Salmon River in Idaho became part of my life in a strange way. Idamae's death was early in 1994. When my friend Dave Jessup began putting together a group of ten for trip, he and his wife Mary felt it would be a good getaway for me as well. Here is a glimpse of this very rigorous adventure.

Each morning after we struck camp and loaded all gear onto the oar boats, Shannon, a 24-year-old college girl and head honcho of the guides, would outline our day: where the stops would be, the rivers that would flow into our river, how difficult the rapids would be, and what historic spot or hot spring we would be stopping at. Each day a different guide would read an article or tell a river story about the wilderness we were floating through.

On the Fourth of July, I presented flags to our guides, big flags for the oar boats and tiny ones to the Michigan contingent. I then made a smart decision—to put my fishing gear away. I could always fish at home, but having a fishing pole prevented me from getting the really good pictures that I had come to get.

The next day I chose to get into an inflatable kayak about 10 feet long. Now this was different. No wetsuit. You just were all wet. We followed one paddle boat, and a second paddle boat followed the four kayaks.

Haystack Rapid had been my goal from the planning of the trip, and it was a "hum dinger!" Here's how you do it: Enter the rapid on the V-slick located 45 feet from the right bank. Once past the submerged boulder, pull to the left of the left half of the river, enabling you to pass through a narrow slot between the boulder bar on the left half of the river and the two midstream boulders located 40 feet apart. Once past the second midstream boulder, position three feet to another boulder located 40 feet below. This enables you to avoid a large midstream boulder by passing to its left. (Here is where I messed up and ran smack dab onto the lower edge of the boulder. Thank goodness I had enough arm strength to push the kayak and me off the boulder.)

I had been in this kayak since after breakfast (time out for lunch), and I was getting very tired. I yelled to Shannon and asked to get into an oar boat to rest. I was afraid my exhaustion might cause me to make a stupid blunder. Mary Jessup was anxious to change places with me, and I could catch a breather. A Motrin 600 helped ease the pains of this day, and it was easy to get to sleep.

As we selected places to set up our individual tents in a crowded camp that evening, a 14-year-old boy named Chris and I stepped simultaneously into a good tent spot. "It's mine!" he yelled.

"Chris, did we both arrive at the same time?"

"Well, yes."

I found a small flat stone and spit on one side of it. As I tossed it into the air, I called out, "Chris, dry or wet?"

"Dry," he yelled.

As it hit the sand spit side up, I started to set up my tent. Chris looked for another spot.

The last night was the kind like you'd wished it would last forever. Supper was fruit juices and parts of fresh fruit, New York strip steaks, and halibut grilled to your wishes. Lots of other goodies, it was and topped off with a pineapple upside-down cake. I was gaining weight. The evening waxed mellow with group singing accompanied by guitar and mouth organs.

From the Riverbank
March 29, 1995

Dipping for Smelt

In April and May, Great Lakes smelt swim upstream, and fishermen grab their large nets on long poles to "dip" them from cold, clear streams. Night dipping yields the best catches. Pan-fried smelt, eaten bones and all, is a tasty treat. When does an avid fisherman ever dip his limit?

Seeing such a beautiful past couple of weeks makes me think of possible early spawning runs of suckers, mullet, and smelt. We once lived in the Upper Peninsula, in the small town of Rapid River. This was in 1949 and 1950. One of the reasons for moving to the Upper Peninsula was the excellent fishing. There was always a season of some kind going on. First walleye and pike season, then partridge and rabbit seasons, followed by duck and goose, and then deer season. It seemed that every weekend I was involved in one of those seasons.

Our first children were about three and six then, and we were expecting our third child. I remember so clearly Idamae asking, "Are there any more seasons coming?" I realized how careless I had been and promised, "No more game or fish seasons until the ice goes out and the smelt begin to run." That seemed like a safe enough promise to make, and I kept it too.

The trouble was that the smelt began to run early that year, so I had to get into the action. What to do with all the smelt? There was a place in Gladstone (only a few miles to the south) that would buy all the smelt you could haul in, and lots of people filled utility trailers and sold them there. I had more modest goals. A fellow teacher and I brought in several garbage pails filled with smelt plus many bags also. The going price was only about three cents a pound, but even that started to add up. My friend Jim didn't want the few dollars that was his part of the take, so he gave me his share. All at once the light bulb went on as to how the proceeds could be put to work! I had an old flat-bottom boat, and now this bonanza became the down payment on a Gamble Store Hiawatha outboard motor. I could hardly wait until the ice left the mill pond so I could try out this powerful 1.5 horsepower motor.

Remember the cartoon "Priscilla and Her Pop"? Pop took mashed potatoes sandwiches in his lunch for years until he could put the down payment for his outboard into action. Well, even if I could dip for smelt here, if and when they showed up in the small feeder streams along Lake Huron, there are no longer places that one can commercially sell hand-dipped smelt. However, I can look forward to those balmy nights in May when it might be fun to dip a small pail full of smelt.

From the Riverbank
August 1, 1995

Tweed I

Every fisherman needs a boat, and I didn't have one. Here is the story of my first one.

Our family had just moved to Rapid River, Michigan, where I had inked a contract to teach in the Rapid River Rural Agricultural School. Three years of college at Michigan State Normal School (now Eastern University) and an additional year at the U of M had made me decide to get into the Upper Peninsula where there was some good fishing. Rapid River looked like a good fishing hole, so I accepted a job there.

Yes, the fish were there, but I was up the river with neither oar nor boat. My dad was sure I really needed a boat but didn't come out and say he would pay for one. I shopped around and found a used one with one side slightly longer than the other (might go in large circles), but it was sturdy and the price was right—$25. I really needed a new suit or at least a pair of trousers, but I spent the $25 on the boat instead. My wife was a good sport. She bought a bottle of strawberry pop and christened it "Tweed" for the clothing that I didn't get.

Tweed never left the head of the mill pond. For one thing, it was too heavy to move. The fishing was so good in the mill pond, the Rapid River, the Whitefish River, and Little Bay De Noc that there never was a question of moving it. I didn't have a trailer as well. Tweed was the ideal boat, too heavy for anyone to even consider stealing yet big enough for our then family of four.

After three years of living in Rapid River and Escanaba and enjoying excellent fishing, it was time to move to Alpena to enjoy a better teaching position. It was tough to think of leaving Tweed and the fishing and hunting. I placed an ad in the Escanaba paper, and it was answered by Clint Dunathon, the paper's editor. It seems that he had an old clunker of a rowboat by the name of Prince Albert, so named for the many small patches cut from Prince Albert tobacco cans and glued and nailed to stop the leaks. Tweed looked good by comparison, and a deal was struck—$25!

The Dunathon kids were excited about their "new" boat. We'd had three years with a good old fishing boat, and the net cost was $0.00. Couldn't ask for a better deal.

By the time I paid my fuel bill, moving expenses, etc., I had no money left to think of buying another boat and no time either. I was lucky getting a job at Huron Hardware in Alpena to help tide us over until our first paycheck from the Alpena Public Schools in October of 1952.

This was only the beginning of the Tweed line. I'll be sharing about Tweed II and some others of the long line of boats carrying the name Tweed.

From the Riverbank
August 8, 1995

Tweed II

Our next boat, Tweed II, was a beauty. Here is her story.

The Tweed dynasty began in the Upper Peninsula in 1949. Tweed I was sold and left behind as our family moved to Alpena in 1952. Tweed II became a constant thought, and in the early spring of 1953, she appeared in a Sears catalog. "Easy to assemble, twelve-foot plywood boat kit, $69.50." It didn't take long to make up my mind that here was the great replacement boat, and at a price that I could handle. Probably had $75 into it with shipping, sales tax, and a few miscellaneous items.

Most of the parts were pre-cut and well identified, and the instructions left no doubt that A and A went together, B and B, and so on. Actually a blind man could have assembled it, and it went together reasonably well. Not quite enough waterproof glue, but Mike's Hardware had that item. When completed, what a beauty! Three coats of spar varnish made the marine plywood glisten, and you could see the matching numbers and numerals that helped make the assembly easy.

Tweed II had great lines, and rowing it was a pleasure. The kids found it easy to maneuver, and with a 3-horsepower motor, it really moved. If it had a watery home, I suppose it was Clear Lake (just north of Atlanta), where we camped for years and years. Tweed II helped keep the family happy with before breakfast and late evening fishing for me and a boy or two and shallow water "puddling" for kids during the day. A quiet row or a sedate motor trip around the lake was Idamae's choice.

The thousands of miles Tweed II was trailered and the hundreds of lakes and streams she graced through the years would be difficult to enumerate: Canadian backwoods, Upper Peninsula lakes, potholes, streams, as well as the three largest of the Great Lakes. Perhaps the most harrowing encounter was in Lake Michigan off the Platte River in October of 1967. I solo fished for salmon in the same water that seven fishermen met their watery death that wild day. I was too dumb to get off the bay until the Coastguard chased me off the water. Lucky day. Some of the most pleasant experiences were drifting down the Pigeon and the Black Rivers with Idamae and Dale.

Time took its toll, and it was 1970 and Tweed II was 17 years old. Paint covered the varnish, and then fiberglass on seams rescued it for a few more years. As more fiberglass and paint were applied, it became heavier and lost some of its grace in the water. Left in the Thunder Bay River all fall as a salmon boat, it was in rough shape when it returned to the house in November. Setting outside another winter didn't improve it. But I did some minor repairs, and it went back to the river in August of 1971.

It was a real pleasure to row up beyond the paper mill and still collect a few salmon, but December, I knew Tweed II would not make it back again. So with ax and saw, I reduced it to small pieces and pitched it into the maw of a waiting garbage truck. Tweed II was gone! But the countless pictures will always endear her to our memory.

From the Riverbank
October 18, 1996

Contrails and Turkey Landings

It seemed that we lived in a paradise between sky and land.

One of the special things about clear skies is that it becomes quite easy to find the contrails traced across the sky by jet planes. I suppose I have a "love affair" with those condensed vapor trails. Whenever I hear the sound of jets, I crane my neck to search for the contrail and the jet plane itself. Where do they come from? Where are they going? I quickly think. "This one on a north by northwest heading, probably left Detroit Metro for a Minneapolis landing; this other one possibly left O'Hare with an overseas destination." Some days the sky seems laced together with fading contrails.

My front yard is used as a landing and take-off field for some local turkeys. The late evening congregation looks for scraps of food, sunflower seeds, bugs, and seeds from the spruce trees. They seem to get antsy, and finally they take off to roost in trees across the river, their silhouettes visible until it really gets dark. The early morning flight lands in twos and threes, touching down and running a few feet to gain balance. Then follow the rituals of flapping wings and stretching to overcome the cramped body positions during their overnight roost. The immature birds horse around and then search for food as the light gets better. Finally, they move to my garden area that I keep raked, staying there until all of the small area is covered with their footprints. Finally, as it becomes truly light, the flock leaders (old, mature hens) lead the flock off to explore other food sources. The Wildlife O'Hare Field is closed until evening shadows return.

From the Riverbank
November 8, 1996

Eagles and Turkeys

Eagles and turkeys are frequent visitors to our area.

A mature bald eagle lifted off from a field just a couple of hundred feet from Black River Road and landed in a nearby tree. Pulling off the road, I got my small camera from the trunk of the car. Of course the eagle flew, but just across the road, so again I thought I could stalk it to get a closer picture. This time when it flew, I lost all sight of it. I suspect there was a road-killed wild animal in the field, and I had disturbed the eagle as it was eating. I should have walked into the field to try to find the source of the eagle's interest. What is great is that so close to home, the eagle still shows up quite frequently.

* * *

The turkeys that were regularly frequenting the neighborhood disappeared a little over two weeks ago. Where did they go? I don't know enough about wild turkeys to figure that one out. But as I drove into my yard early this week, there 18 of them were finishing up on some whole corn that had been spread before the snow had fallen, now melted. Is their sense of smell so good that they could detect corn from a long distance?

* * *

Weather predictions are for the experts, and wooly-bear caterpillars just don't cut it. However, attitudes about the weather and seasons are another whole story. The other day was rather nice, possibly a bit overcast, but still nice. I conveyed this thought about the day to a fellow shopper.
"But it might rain or snow this afternoon," was the reply.

So there you are. One saw it as having the sun almost come out, even if it just showed a warm, yellow disc where it might come out; another saw the possibility of rain and snow. For some, winter is already in their mind and further depressing them, while others can think of the silver lining possibilities. So goes life, and hopefully we run into more optimists than pessimists.

Not on the Road
March 31, 1993

Nature in the Raw

The signs of life are sometimes struggles.

Bits of fur and blood on the snow under our bird feeder alerted me to investigate. The hair looked like that of a cottontail rabbit, but there were no predator footprints in the snow; so who was the attacker? Wing feather imprints told me part of the story. An owl had swooped down and grabbed the rabbit as it was eating bird food during the night. Marks of a struggle told me the rabbit tried to run.

The owl pulled the rabbit about ten feet to the edge of the bank. It then became airborne, rabbit and all, but the load was too heavy. Back to the ground. There the owl killed the rabbit, opened the upper chest (from the back), and ate until satisfied. It then severed the head from the body. Hiding the rest of the carcass in a brush pile, it flew off with the head. The next morning, the rest of the rabbit was gone. The crows came in and did the clean-up job.

In the 1930s, a billboard on M-95 (now 211) proclaimed, "Nature in the raw is seldom mild." Old-timers may recognize this slogan as part of a Lucky Strike ad. Its message still rings true.

From the Riverbank
Date Unknown

Fishers and Birders

Traditions of family and friends are life training experiences, and they make rich memories.

Another opening of trout season has come and gone. This one was truly for the hardy souls that could put up with ice in the pole guides, chill in their veins, and very cold fingers. But there were fish to be caught if one found the right place and could tough it out.

I made my annual stop by the warm fire and hot coffee and sticky buns at the Chapman Crockett Rapids outing. My opening day was a real success just having spent some time visiting with old friends and renewing acquaintances. And that is the great thing about it: an extended family getting together to carry on a tradition. Small kids running all over the place, old-timers soaking up the heat of the fire and food, and then the in-between generations that make it all come together. For someone who didn't even buy a fishing license yet, I have had a successful season opener.

This past weekend was another very special event in the lives of some specialized out-of-door people. The hawk migration is underway, and Whitefish Point in the Upper Peninsula is the action spot. As hawks and other migratory birds move northward through Michigan, comes a time when they always stop, rest, and possibly think about the crossing to Canada. Wind and atmospheric pressures have something to due with the decision to cross or to delay for a few hours or possibly the next day. But the birders can't delay; they must be there when the decisions are made. Birders from all over, dressed for the weather (good or bad) and with binoculars, field guides, and checklists, are ready for whatever species are making the crossing to Canada.

Whitefish Point is a visiting spot for tourists with their children, dogs, and the trailered boats during the warm summer, but it is a different story now. Quite a lot of RV units show up. Self-contained is the way to go. It doesn't take long for the brisk wind to chill one to the bone, and how nice to duck into the warm RV for a coffee and a warm-up.

Why would anyone be at Whitefish Point at this time of the year? Hawks! The northward migration is on, and this is one place to really see them. Their movement through the sky, from south to north, is in a slowly turning circular pattern called kettling. If it is a good day, you might see several hawks of differing kinds make the crossing. Often a large flock of robins may be crossing with dozens of the small merlins as well as blue jays. Sometimes the wind changes or becomes too strong, and the birds turn around before getting to the halfway point and return to set out again a few minutes or hours later.

The birders are in a festive mood when the migration is strong. Everyone keeps his or her Audubon Bird Count cards on the ready and records species as well as numbers. Some real learning takes place, as a pro may shout, "There's a sharp-shined among that group of red tails!" The field glasses or spotting scopes try to find the group and the unusual or atypical hawk.

There is a real thrill being on hand to see the hawks make this crossing and continue their migration. So if someone says they have been to Whitefish Point during late April or early May, they really aren't nuts; they just may be birders.

From the Riverbank
December 29, 1993

Camping in Pigeon River Country

Beautiful bird songs stir a heart to see glory.

The river is a thing of real beauty this Christmas morning! Ice has inched out from both banks eight or ten feet, leaving an opening of nearly ten feet. Snow and ice leisurely move downstream, and snow covers everything else in this study of black and white. Only rabbit and squirrel tracks add to the scene. If the weather stays cold for another few days, the Black will be totally frozen over.

Sometimes it takes winter to remind us of spring, and I'd like to share a memory of a campout along the Pigeon River one late April. The sun had set, and the afterglow had vanished. Dusk left soft tones and winnowing woodcocks, the drumming of partridges, and the late evening songs of the robins. Missing was the whip-poor-will and the night hawks. Just a week or two too soon for them. Night moved in with a lull of rippling stream noises, a thunder and lightning storm to the northwest, and a few owl hoots mixed in. Z ... Z ... Z ... Into the arms of Morpheus.

A brown thrasher almost on top of the camper was my morning wake-up call, and then the spring chorus. The stake-driving, pump-pulsing sounds of the American bittern, red-winged blackbirds chirring, plaintive song of the wood thrush mixed in with harsh kingfisher and blue jay talk; and accentuating all was the woodpecker clan banging away with drumming that sounded like it was just for the fun of it.

Creeping quietly from the camper, I took a long walk downstream into God's country. Really a bit of heaven revisited, possibly a new corner of paradise missed until now. Lungs filled with the smell of pungent leaf decay and the perfume of trailing arbutus. I breakfasted on four wintergreen berries that satisfied. As I climbed my hill to look over my kingdom, the chorus of peeper frogs diminished, and the truly day sounds took over as the song sparrow added its melody to the thrashers and morning robins. It was sun up.

As I have been musing and writing, the Black River has slowed, and now ice and snow plug most of the channel. How different the scene! Change seems to be the only constant.

From the Riverbank
January 24, 1997

Naming a Bird

Naming a creature connects one to creation.

A junco has been a regular customer at my bird feeder for many weeks. But why would a junco linger on in this north country well beyond the time that others of its family have headed to warmer climes? We watched as this somewhat dumpy appearing bird came early each morning, and ignoring the chickadees, just "hung in there." For some reason, possibly a brush with a predator, it just needed a place to recuperate.

Each morning as daylight approached, I trained my field glasses on the feeder to see if "Junco" (now it had a special name) came in to feed. Last Saturday morning, with the temperature minus 26° below zero, sure enough, there was Junco. But what a bedraggled sight it was, and it appeared to have a disabled leg.

We grieved for it and looked in vain for it the next morning. I tried to think what I might have looked like if I had been the one to spend that horribly cold night outside. However, Monday morning with somewhat warmer temperatures, there was Junco once again, feeding as usual. This is a special bird at our feeder, and we are rooting for it to safely survive the rigors of winter and be well rested and ready to join the migrating flocks of juncos as they pass through here in late March or early April.

* * *

We look out over the frozen Black River at mealtimes and see lots of "snow snakes" on bare branches and frequently the two male cardinals that we have come to call "our cardinals."

"I think I see a big woodpecker with a red head!" The ever-present field glasses verify that indeed it is a big woodpecker. The male pileated is systematically probing the bark of some trees about 100 yards away. How great to have such a splendid visitor at our Sunday noon meal!

We have both scanned that same bunch of trees just on the off chance that the pileated might have returned. Since a pair of pileated annually raises a clutch of young in this immediate area, I'm sure the bird has a secure site to get out of the rigors of snow and ice. The pileated is the size of a crow, and when in flight, a distinct patch of white is visible. Its flight is distinctly undulating, as with all members of the woodpecker family. When I hear the first calls of the flicker, I must remember that it probably is the pileated instead.

From the Riverbank
April 2, 1996

Smoked Fish Flavored Raisins

I love raisins, and I discovered that turkeys and robins do too.

I love the big raisins that are sold in bulk packages at area grocery stores! Those bran and wheat cereals that boast of two scoops of raisins in every package don't say how big the scoop is. I load each bowl of my cereal with a big handful of monster raisins.

Something happened recently when I took a 5-pound package of raisins from the garage freezer and dumped a handful on some cereal. How could this be? The raisins had a distinct smoked fish odor to them! I like smoked fish and certainly raisins, but not mixed together. It seems that my son Paul had caught some nice steelhead and brown trout. After Paul smoked them, I placed them in packages in the freezer. Either they were very strong flavored or poorly wrapped fish (possibly both), and the raisins picked up the smoked fish flavor.

I thought of tossing them into the garbage can, but no. Just maybe squirrels or opossum might eat them. So I scattered them on the front lawn. Sunday morning, the "Three Stooges" were busily eating them. These turkeys enjoy sunflower seeds, but that day they preferred the raisins. Then "Robin Redbreast" started pecking at the raisins. What a sight until the snow storm covered the food. I knew robins liked to eat frozen apples left on trees over winter, so I suppose the fruity smell of raisins attracted it. I strung up some prunes on a thin wire and hung them on a small mountain ash tree, hoping that Robin would return. Sure enough, last Wednesday Robin was back, and not finding the raisins, sought out the prunes. I can't buy raisins at $1.59 per pound to feed these birds.

* * *

Someone asked me if I had seen the comet. Actually, I had watched the diagrams on TV reports that clearly spelled and pronounced the name but ignored all of it because the nights seemed to be too cloudy. But these very cold nights (and incidentally very clear nights) were just the ticket to look for the comet. How lucky! As I opened my back door, which faces the east, there staring me in the face was the comet. I have searched through lots of newspapers yet have not found one with the name of that elusive heavenly body.

I recall my mother talking about Halley's Comet and what a great thrill it was for her to see it. I must admit my memory is a total flop, and I must still search for the name of this most recent comet.

From the Riverbank
May 14, 1995

Signs of the Season

One can mark time by noting nature's visitors.

"Spring is bustin' out all over" just like the lyrics from *Oklahoma*. My early morning walk was beautiful with the songs of the robins, rose-breasted grosbeaks, ovenbirds, yellow-bellied sapsuckers, white crown and white throat sparrows, plus the splash of colors as the orioles came in to drink from the ruby-throated hummingbird's feeder. Hummingbirds are also here and in need of nectar until enough flowers are in bloom.

This is a spring full of birds, but I wait to announce summer until the indigo bunting, brown thrasher, and catbird take up residence. A male prothonotary warbler is just now exploring the bushes along the opposite bank of the river. This is a rare find for me.

To the more practical signs of spring, the black fly is just now asserting its ownership of the out-of-doors. Mosquitoes can't be far behind. If this is the price of spring, so be it.

From the Riverbank
June 28, 1995

Turkey Trot

Nature's ways are often ahead of our perceptions.

One of strangest sights met my eyes Wednesday morning as I looked out my kitchen window! A "Jake" turkey was moving from south to north, toward the river, and just behind it were five other turkeys, all at a slow "turkey trot."

What was seemingly herding them? As I looked farther to the south, there was "Bun-Bun," the tame rabbit that thinks she owns my total yard. She was doing the "bunny hop" just fast enough to keep six turkeys trotting. Oh, for a video cam! As I made a dash to get the nearest camera, the turkeys broke formation and made an escape into the next door neighbor's lot.

My next question was, what caused Bun-Bun to do the fast bunny hop? A few minutes later, I heard the barking of a dog. It had probably smelled all this game, and being a city dog, didn't quite know what to do with more game than it had ever encountered at reasonably close range. The Jakes were gone, and Bun-Bun, being close to me, decided to beg for a salty cracker.

From the Riverbank
January 10, 1997

Winter's Beauty Arrives

The hazards of winter driving in our area are surpassed in magnitude only by the beauty.

If there is any doubt that winter has truly arrived, just look about you. My snow blower has been busy, and I have seen many roofs that have required snow removal. The cruelest blow has been the ice-covered trees plus the winds that brought down power lines. A truly hard hit area included the Golden Beach Manor on Lake Huron. Although portable generators kept the heat on and the food from thawing in the freezers, a real scarcity of water proved to be a hardship. The P. I. E. & G. crews have worked around the clock to repair the damage.

Returning from Cheboygan Tuesday afternoon presented a spectacular view of winter beauty. The ice-covered trees towards Mullet Lake were a fairyland of crystal. Some roads also seemed to be more than just a bit nasty. However, both the Presque Isle and Cheboygan road crews did a fine job of clearing, grading, and salting the roads. The salt quota for January has been heavily used. May we hope for better weather for the next number of weeks?

* * *

My ash tree took considerable damage by yellow-bellied sapsuckers the past two summers, leaving not too much green branches and fewer fruit. I considered getting out the chainsaw and start all over. However, a family conference decided that this tree must stay. It is the ideal landing spot for the many cardinals, goldfinches, and a few purple finches. They stop in the ash tree before lighting on or in one of the bird feeders. This is their tree and the place we can get the best view of these and other birds.

From the Riverbank
November 15, 1996

Stoves on the Hearth

Heating our homes over the years has presented many challenges.

Moving to the Riverhouse in 1977 changed my way of thinking about being prepared for winter. Just keeping the buried oil tank filled monthly was all that was required at 2970 Ontario Street in Alpena. The story changed upon moving here, when not only was it necessary to keep the oil barrel filled and the LP tanks replenished, but there was that gaping face of a garage-like building that needed to be filled with wood. It was a balancing act to try to keep a small home warm with two oil space heaters and a zero clearance fireplace. Lots of exercise carrying wood, as the fireplace was good looking but didn't produce enough heat to warrant taking up that much space. Eventually the fireplace became a hearth to support a long line of wood stoves that also burned nine or ten cords of wood each winter and still didn't really keep the house warm.

The next heating device was a wall-hung furnace that was small enough to fit into the pantry and heated 40 feet of baseboard finned radiators. A Quadrafire wood stove seemed the final evolution of stoves, but still the necessity of either getting up my own wood or buying ten cords.

Now, however, a very pretty stove sits on the hearth, and the flames come and go as the thermostat wills. Now all I have to do is to keep my gas bills paid. The gaping hole of the woodshed is now plugged with a boat and a fold-down camper plus other odds and ends. I truly enjoyed the neatly stacked piles of firewood and the smells of many kinds of wood. Possibly this is progress, and I know back pains are fewer; but somehow I feel as if I have sold out, and my current type of heating is no longer that of the good old days.

From the Riverbank
January 10, 1996

Snow Adventures for Grandkids

Visits from grandkids are especially memorable when the heavy snows are here.

"Grandpa, will there be enough snow at your house?" I quickly assured the grandchildren that there would indeed be plenty of snow for any activity when they would arrive.

One of the first ventures was to build an igloo. Lots of fun and quite sturdy, with a roof supported with boards. Then came the snow picnics. Packing the car with five pairs of snowshoes plus two plastic sleds was a start. The picnic basket was loaded with hot dogs and buns, hot chocolate and coffee, and an assortment of Christmas cookies. We were ready to head for Tomahawk Floodings.

The picnic came first, and soon a just-right fire for roasting hot dogs was ready. We didn't have to worry about the fire spreading this day. Deep and powdery snow made both sledding and snowshoeing difficult, but we toughed it out. The toasty warm house was pleasant to return to. The grandkids begged to have another picnic the very next day, and it was decided that the triple culverts on the Pigeon River would be our destination.

Hard-packed snowmobile trails made it easy to get from the Osmun Road to our picnic location. Many chickadees joined us, sitting on our caps and backs as well as eating crumbs from the hands of the grandkids. This was the kids' very first experience of having a wild bird be so tame. I was chief fire tender, soaking up the heat and pungent smoke odors, while the rest of the crew went sledding on an untraveled road.

As the family left for home, they were totally satisfied with the amount of snow in the Onaway area. Their enthusiasm got me "into the act" and caused me to plan yet another winter picnic to be enjoyed the very next day. Three winter cookout picnics in four days may set some sort of a record. I do know that they help make the winter more fun.

Not on the Road
March 31, 1993

Substitute Teacher Days

Generations can bridge the divide.

Retiring from school teaching in 1977, I couldn't remotely think of myself as a substitute teacher. Yet it happened. I was bored with too much spare time, so when Caroline Pregitzer needed someone to "sub" for the Onaway elementary grades, I helped out when needed.

One day I showed up in a third grade classroom. The teacher had prepared the children that they would have a man teacher on Monday. As I chatted with a few children before school, Donnie Hoffmeyer came in. He walked around me two or three times and then said, "I didn't think you would be this old!"

He took me by surprise, so I said, "Donnie, I have two granddaughters, one in Cincinnati and one in Alpena. They are in the third grade. Do you think I'm old enough to be a grandfather? He agreed that I was, and the crisis was defused.

One of the lasting joys of having been a sub in Onaway schools was to meet the grandchildren of the people I grew up with. It still gives me a warm feeling to be able to recognize some of Onaway's now not-so-young teachers. I have been told, "You can always tell a teacher, but you can't tell them much."

From the Riverbank
April 30, 1999

Mole Holes

Of all the critters that live among us, moles may be the least appreciated. The Riverhouse yard had an overabundance.

Moles have really been active, even throughout the winter, and there is no secret as to where they have been working. The unsightly piles of earth that dot lawns seem to be the extra soil the moles push up when their underground tunnels get too full. This brings up the question as to why they are there in the first place. They do eat worms and night crawlers, but there is a more succulent creature of the sod that is the major target, and that is the large, white grub of the June bug beetle.

You must see the mole to appreciate how it can do all of this underground mischief. It is quite big, about six or seven inches long, and it is no lightweight, with a body mass larger than that of a big red squirrel. The nose is long and pointed, with whiskers to help probe its underground meals. A smallish mouth is studded with needle-like teeth. As to eyes, it is difficult to locate them, as most of what it does is underground, where good eyesight really isn't necessary. Next comes the very muscular shoulders and a pair of front feet that are enormous for an animal of its size.

This is a digging machine beyond compare. The front legs remove the soil from places that the nose and probing hairs tell the body to go, and the diminutive hind legs help propel the mole forward. If a tree root or a stone lies in the path, a change of direction takes place.

I borrowed a mole trap just to see if I could catch a mole. While waiting for the trap to produce a dead mole (it hasn't happened yet), I fired up my rototiller. Lo and behold, the rototiller got the first mole! Here was a real digger that out-dug a big mole! I'm still waiting for the trap to spring underground and spear the culprit.

There is a competitor for the big, white grubs, and it too produces lots of holes in the lawn. I'm speaking of the skunk. However, skunks work from the top side, digging dozens of small holes to capture their meals. Just can't win! What grubs the skunks don't get, the moles come along to complete the damage.

From the Riverbank
June 7, 1995

Fruit Trees Required

Fresh fruit from a tree in the yard is almost a requirement for our family!

Plant some fruit trees just as soon as you move to a new location. This good bit of advice came from my grandfather, John Fairman, to my father, Oscar Roberts. Ontario Street in Alpena was where I planted our first apple trees. But first I had 40 yards of rich clay-loam soil brought to cover the sandy soil that covered my yard. This became a great garden, and friends would compliment me on it while complaining about how poorly their garden was. A few dwarf apple trees grew as well.

When we moved to Cope Road, a swamp greeted us. It required lots of work with the chainsaw to open a spot that would let sunshine in. Having to install a raised septic system opened the land up for more light, but the real problem was lack of productive soil. When Billy Mann and his father installed the septic system, they brought in about six inches of topsoil from an active alfalfa field. Now I was ready to plant some apple trees!

There was only room for three, and a family conference voted for a Transparent, a McIntosh, and a Golden Delicious. The Transparent soon died, but the McIntosh and Delicious did quite well. The McIntosh produced less and less until one fall I whispered to it that it had only one more season if it didn't "shape up." I relented, and another season of very poor apples (about two dozen) sealed its doom.

The Delicious flourished and produced tart-sweet flavor apples in the late fall. But something in the soil started the same slowdown in it that overcame the other trees. When I was ready to prune this last tree, it became apparent that it would produce no blossoms. Out came the chainsaw. It hadn't heard my whispered threat to the McIntosh! Actually I felt sad but had to do it.

Do I plant another tree and hope for it to live long enough to reap a harvest? Of course! Grandchildren and great grandchildren can enjoy the fresh apples, and I also plan to enjoy some of the sweet-tart of the Golden Delicious.

From the Riverbank
September 3, 1999

Remembering Maybell's Flowers

Learning to love natural things such as flowers is a gift from our elders.

My mother, Maybell Roberts, lived across from Edna Lound's store, and she always had a yard full of flowers from early spring until late fall. Mom worked tirelessly in her garden and would rather spend money on bulbs and plants than decorations within her home. Out-of-town visitors would make the short detour from State Street to drink in the beauty of her flower garden. Mom had great flower gardens when we lived beside the elevator, but it was too far off the beaten path for many to enjoy.

My brothers and I were introduced into the art of proper spading, weeding, and watering that helped Mother produce her excellent flowers. Mother also won many awards for flower arranging. She fixed floral pieces on Saturday afternoon, and my dad carried them to the Methodist Church early Sunday morning to be altar pieces. Many shut-ins also enjoyed Mom's flowers and her artistic arrangements.

From the Riverbank
February 15, 1995

No Place Like Home

A warm wood stove, a plowed driveway, and seed catalogs make a welcome homecoming.

Yes, I'm back and keeping the home fires burning. When I left home before Christmas, it seems that I was very tired or a "bug" of some kind latched onto me. Since my plans were already made, I was determined to keep my commitment to work with the Nomads in Leesburg, Florida.

As my first work session neared completion and it was time to move south to Alva, Florida, my energy level was totally zapped. I visited a doctor and was advised to return home and truly rest up. At the evening meal, my friends asked what the doctor had said. Trying to pull some humor from the situation, I said, "My doctor said, 'Mylanta.'" We all had a good laugh, and the next morning I packed up and left for the Riverbank.

My son Paul had turned on my furnace, lit the wood stove, turned on the water, and plowed the driveway. I returned to a cozy home, even though it was quite cold outside. Lots of rest plus medication are doing wonders, and I'm back on the recovery path.

The flood of seed catalogs continues to show up. I'm glad no one told them I didn't plant a garden last year. I need the bright pictures of both flowers and vegetables to warm my thoughts of spring and summer. A newcomer, at least to me, entitled Pine-Tree Garden Seeds, showed up in the mail recently. The catalog states the company's philosophy in three words: "Selection" (over 750 varieties of seeds); "Quality" (an ironclad promise to perform) or your money back; and "Price" (always reasonable). Now if this gardener prepares the soil well, follows good gardening practices, frost stays away, and the sun shines (this list is already getting longer than can be honestly promised for most of our spring and summer seasons), something good has to happen. I'm ready and waiting to get my garden planned and planted.

From the Riverbank
Date Unknown

The River Ice Breakup

Keeping track of river conditions makes for expected and unexpected observations.

Do rabbits swim? Not unless they have to!

My early morning routine includes checking and recording the temperature, barometric pressure, sky, and condition of the river. Water had started to cover parts of the ice about a week ago. As I looked across the river on Tuesday morning, there was a commotion on the far side. A small beaver? A duck? I grabbed the field glasses, and it was a large cottontail rabbit attempting to cross the river on its regular ice and snow path to get a breakfast of corn. But now, with three to five inches of water flowing on top of the ice, it was another situation.

Brer Rabbit was determined, and probably frightened as well. It hopped, jumped, and swam until it reached the south bank. The bedraggled rabbit looked like a small dog shaking water from its fur. Yes, a rabbit can swim in ice-cold water if the incentives are strong enough.

Wednesday morning's check of the river condition suggested that the breakup would he soon. I hoped the ice wouldn't go out in the night, as watching a breakup is always exciting. Thursday morning was the time of breakup. A sizeable ice jam kept growing out in front. For the next hour and a half, huge blocks of ice from upstream added to the jam. Some of the smaller pieces (3 feet by 6 feet or so) would slide under the face of the ice jam, and I could hear them bump, grind, and scrape as they slid under the solid ice downstream. Some really big floes, up to 8 feet by 20 feet, would crash into the jam and would either break up or slide under, making a crashing noise. This was thick ice, six to ten inches deep. A very large one tipped up at an angle as the leading edge hit the bottom of the river, causing the water to flow on top of the five or six feet high jam of ice. That started the whole mass moving with a grumbling, and down the river it went.

The water level dropped quickly. Within ten minutes, the water level had dropped two feet, and the Black was now running freely. Many floes of varying size continued from above, and it wasn't until noon that the river was totally free of ice. This was one of the best breakup shows I had witnessed in years.

Brer Rabbit may have to wait until the freeze up next winter before crossing back to the north side.

From the Riverbank
June 11, 1999

Observations of Flora and Fauna

Here is a collection of observations on flora and fauna.

The hummingbird population seems to be about normal this season, but the nectar in our feeder doesn't disappear as rapidly. I haven't seen as many orioles as usual, and none of them have come to the hummingbird feeder. I usually prepare a quart of sweet water at a time for it, and since the feeder only holds a cup of liquid, the rest goes into the refrigerator. (Sweet water goes cloudy if it is kept too long at room temperature.) Filling the feeder this very hot morning, I was tempted to hang around the window and wait for the first hummer to show up and shiver as the first sip was taken, possibly thinking, "I didn't know it was that cold last night."

* * *

Driving the north border of Black River Ranch on the late evening of June 1, we saw a deer leaving the center of the road. A small object about the size of a jack rabbit required that I turn left to avoid hitting it. A wise decision, because when we stopped the object, turned out to be a just born fawn. It made the very wobbly attempt to stand and finally got to the side of the road. Not wishing to disturb it, we drove on a hundred feet or so and watched as the mother deer came back to the newborn fawn. We hoped that a coyote didn't come upon the scene before the doe and fawn could seek a more secluded hiding spot.

* * *

Mushroom hunting hadn't been good, and as I was walking back to where I had parked, a movement on my right captured my attention. It looked as if a very large snapping turtle had just settled down to avoid being detected. Slowly walking toward the spot, I was surprised to see a big hen turkey squatting on the ground, obviously covering a clutch of eggs. Luckily I had my camera along, and I sneaked ever closer. The turkey ignored me completely, as if her camouflage was so complete that I couldn't see her. Lying down on the ground next to her, I was able to shoot some eggs protruding from under her body and zero in at very close range. She never blinked her eyes as I clicked off many pictures. I then left quietly so as to not disturb her. I still have that sequence of slides that I treasure. A week later I tried to find the nesting site, but to no avail.

From the Riverbank
May 28, 1999

The Clam and the Water Beetle

The relationship of the water level to the life of the critters that inhabit the shore is a delicate balance.

The water level of Black Lake was noticeably lower after the last of the ice had gone. Repairs to Alverno Dam required a lowering the water level, and with little or no rain in April, sand bars showed up. Clams didn't respond to the lowered water level, so major numbers were stranded. Some buried deep into the sand, but some of them seemed to be trapped and destined to die. I heaved many out from their entrapment and wondered at my concern for the lowly clam. Knowing that the clam is and always has been an integral part of the lake ecology, it just felt right to help preserve part of the whole.

While so involved, I saw a rather large, flat water beetle having difficulty maneuvering in the shallow water and took a closer look. An extremely small clam had clamped shut on the left front leg of the beetle. Closer examination of this conjoined pair prompted me to try to release one or both of them. The small clam was so cleverly made that it was impossible to crush it between my thumb and finger. Now what? My pocket knife cut off the portion of the beetle leg grasped by the clam, and both were free. Silly, perhaps, but 24 hours later I observed the same beetle (with shortened leg) moving along as if nothing had happened.

From the Riverbank
August 15, 1995

Losing the Township Dump

Maturity may be owning our own follies.

I've lost a few things in my lifetime, mostly small items like a pocketknife, watch, and other items such as credit cards, wallet, etc., that turned up later. There always seems to be that moment of truth when you realize something isn't where it should be: the extra key that will get you into your car when you see your keys dangling from the ignition of your locked car, or when you reach for your wallet to pay for gas just pumped and have that sinking feeling as you feel your wallet pocket is a flat as a pancake.

But there are larger things that get lost. One time I had accumulated enough garbage to make the usual run and had just enough time to take it to the Forest Township dump before going to the senior citizens supper on the hill. Imagine my total surprise and consternation when I arrived at the dump site and there was nothing there! Not even the fence or a stray scrap of paper to identify it as the dump.

How could I have lost a total half acre dump site? Was I dreaming? Did I make the wrong turn off M-68 in Tower? Needless to say, I was totally puzzled. Probably a notice had appeared in the paper and I had missed it, but surely there would be a sign saying "Township Dump Site Moved to New Location" followed by a map and instructions. But no, just a clean piece of ground!

Well, I was getting hungry and left for supper. "I'll ask someone what had happened," I told myself. When I sat down at a table, I could see no members of Forest Township in my immediate view. Then I spotted Ted Skinner, and I went to where he was seated and got the lowdown. "Why yes, they moved the dump site last week, and if you had been awake and looked, you could have seen it from where you turned around."

I thanked Ted, and on my way home I drove back to the old site and looked almost west a quarter of a mile. There was the lost dump site. I was very glad to get the garbage to the right place, especially since it had started to smell a bit ripe. May I'll never lose another item as big as the Township Dump!

From the River Bank
December 3, 1999

Cranberry Picking

Berry picking of all kinds is a Roberts tradition, and cranberry picking is possibly the most unusual of them all.

Cranberries and Thanksgiving go together like peanut butter and jelly in a good sandwich. But finding the wild cranberries this year was a near impossibility. Water level in the bogs is a critical factor in cranberry culture. The commercial cranberry producers just raise or lower the water in their impoundments to reach the optimum amount of water to produce the good crop.

Looking at the shoreline of any lake or pond tells us that something is wrong. Lakes Michigan and Huron are three to four feet lower than usual, and the bogs that required knee boots to pick the wild berries are dry, grassy fields.

Market cranberries were in abundance, and the price was right. After Thanksgiving the price took a drop, and now the bag that used to be a pound has changed to 12 ounces and sells for about a dollar.

We combine finely chopped oranges (peel and all) with the berries at the ratio of 5 cups of berries to 1 cup of orange, and sugar to taste. We like to keep it on the tart side. Hopefully the water levels will rise by next spring, and we will be able to pick from the bog rather than in the market.

Not on the Road
March 16, 1993

Family Adventures in Winter

Our family started cross-country skiing in 1972. Here is the humble beginning.

As I looked at those low-cut shoes, narrow skis, and bindings, I vowed I wouldn't waste my money on those "sissy-looking" things, so Vern Smith gave me a pair of *real* skis. They were 40 years old, 7 feet long, 4 inches wide, and weighted a ton. I rigged wide inner tube bindings to help keep my sorrel boots in the old toe straps and joined Idamae and Dale in the white stuff.

I bravely set out to break trail for their slim slats. My skis clung to the snow like glue, and it felt like I was wearing 20-pound snowshoes. Eventually I tried Idamae's skis, and came the revelation! I at once sold my 30-06 deer rifle, bought the new equipment, and moved into the real world of XC skiing. We waxed our skis for all conditions, and for about 15 years, we reveled in this exciting winter fun.

After a number of winters spent in the southland, we wondered if we could get back on the thin slats. Yes, everything came back so smoothly. We were lucky that the snow was at winter's best. We don't go to managed or groomed trails but put on our skis at our back door and strike off into the woods, creating our own trails. How great to see the tracks of the mice, squirrels, deer, coyotes, otter, and other animals and birds. A special treat is sucking "sap-cicles" on maple branches. Squirrels and deer nip the ends of the branches, and with the right temperatures, presto-chango: sap-cicles.

* * *

Our daughter, Ann Glawe, celebrated her two birthdays recently. Sound strange? On March 5, 1988, Ann received two pints of bone marrow as a birthday gift from her brother Paul. It was a last, desperate attempt to save her life after an eight-year battle with lymphoma and finally bone cancer. Idamae and I, along with Ann's husband and their youngest daughter, watched as Paul's bone marrow was transfused into Ann. (Paul was missing from this momentous moment in a recovery room two floors below.) This was her second birthday! The miracle took place, and now more than five years later, Ann is enjoying excellent health. We all can't have two birthdays, but we are so thankful that Ann does!

* * *

The sun was shinning brightly on a recent Saturday, and it was just too beautiful to stay inside even though the temperature hovered below 15°. The picnic basket was packed, and off we went to Tomahawk Flooding.

After leaving M-33, the roads were very icy. We found a place protected from the wind but looking out onto the tree-studded ice. The dead lower branches of jack pines made a nice fire, and soon "tube steaks" were sizzling on our sticks while the tailgate became our table. Creole style hot dogs (blackened) on a slab of bread, an apple, a cookie, and tea completed the feast. Nothing like a simple winter picnic to help brighten the day. The weatherman says we can plan on winter picnics for at least a few weeks.

Not on the Road
March 12, 1993

Escaping for the Day

When cabin fever hits, a day trip to another part of our beautiful state is a good cure.

Do you sometimes feel the urge to "escape" for the day? We did this week, and after checking the map to see where and how far to the west shoreline of Michigan, it looked inviting. So I popped a couple of peanut butter sandwiches, bananas, apples, and a jug of water into a brown bag, we were off.

Turning north at Alanson and then west at Brutus, we headed through Stutsmanville and then north on M-119 towards Good Hart. Beautiful sunshine, pristine fields without snowmobile tracks, and very few animal tracks. The music made by moving ice on Lake Michigan was exciting from our vantage point on the road high above the lake.

We drove down to Middle Village and the big church. No sign as to denomination, but it was probably an Indian Catholic, as it was on the site of the first Jesuit Mission in 1741. It was rebuilt by the Indian Village in 1825. We ate our lunch beside the church and then walked down to the sandy shore of Lake Michigan. On to Cross Village and Levering, returning through Cheboygan and then home. This was a day of exploration and beauty, bringing us a bit closer to spring.

* * *

We saw two unusual birds this past week. Three had been killed on our bridge, probably struck by a car as they were getting grit or sand. One was a white-winged crossbill. The female resembles a goldfinch in winter plumage, and the male could be mistaken for a purple finch or a red crossbill. Their winter food consists of seeds from spruce cones and some field weeds. The other unusual bird was a pine siskin that flew into our open screened porch. Such beautiful yellow tail-patches as it "spread-eagled" on the screen.

I carefully picked it up and called Idamae to enjoy its beauty. So tiny, with yellow in its wings plus a needle-sharp beak. The special features of these birds would be lost to field glasses. How fortunate to be able to examine them in our hands.

* * *

Last Tuesday's date, 3-9-93, is a calendar date that will not be repeated, ever! It is called a palendromic number because it is the same whichever way you read it. Last year the palendromic number from the calendar was 2-9-92, and next year it will be 4-9-94. Add this to your store of trivia.

From the Riverbank
November 16, 1994

Backyard Mechanic

Grease monkeys are a vanishing breed.

My back was "ouchy." Then I remembered the previous day I was flat on my back under my truck, changing oil and using the grease gun. Now I ask myself, why? My Scotch blood? Challenge? Possibly both, but it is something I can do! One used to be able to do a lot of repair and maintenance things for our cars, and we felt that we had to just to save money. But the newer "smart cars" defy the backyard mechanic in all ways. Now there is nothing I can do.

In the old car, if the idle was too slow, a screwdriver was all that was needed. Carburetor acting up? An easy job. But now the computer monitors correct it all. A mechanic plugs in a book-sized computer into an outlet under the hood and it reports, "The last 11 starts were perfect." And that's just for starters. These tricky on-board computers make hundreds of decisions and put the corrections into effect each minute. So the era of self-fix has essentially ended.

Now I know why so many older men wander the aisles of K-Mart and Wal-Mart, looking for cases of oil, oil filters, air filters, and more. Being "grease monkeys" is the only thing we can still do for our "steeds," and I'm sure that stiffening, arthritic fingers will eventually rob us even of this job.

From the Riverbank
March 1, 1995

Typewriter to Word Processor

A new day dawned when I engaged a word processor.

March 1, 1995, a new era begins in my writing. Up until now I have used the legal-sized yellow pads, a series of pencils, and naturally, some erasers.

The real problem has been inserting or deleting parts of text. And after completing all the pencil work, I had to set up the typewriter and prepare a copy that was clear and accurate to deliver to *The Outlook*, often late Sunday afternoon or evening but more often early Monday morning.

I made the big plunge and bought a word processor. What fun to apply my clumsy fingers to the delicate keys of this midget of the processor clan. It is quite a bit smaller than my electric typewriter and about a thousand times as smart when I do some wrong things; and believe you me, I can do many wrong things! All one has to do is retype the correct spelling, and presto-chango, the correction is made. I could hardly wait until this article was finished to then use the spelling checker to catch all of the misspelled words. Most times the errors were from hitting the incorrect key.

I have lots of problems trying to get used to the word processor, and I have found it necessary to call a son to help me out of my difficulty. By setting up my small cassette recorder beside the phone, I am able to talk through my problem with Dale and get back on the right track. This also allows me to be in more frequent contact with my family. I'm very pleased that I had the courage to go to this member of the personal computer clan.

From the Riverbank
October 6, 1993

Writer's Block

Few of us know the pressure and pain of writer's block. Sometimes we just punt.

A few weeks ago I lamented the lack of a truly quiet place to collect my thoughts and write this weekly article. I'll let you in on another secret. I found the ideal quiet (well, relatively quiet) place, and the ideas still just don't automatically transfer onto paper!

It's Sunday afternoon, and I'm wondering how I could possibly procrastinate so long. Idamae tells me it's from years and years of practice, but I try to ignore her helpful information. I'm bundled up and sitting in our screened porch overlooking the river. The temperature is 50 degrees with a wild wind blowing. Most of the trees within my view have lost a lot of their leaves, and fall is truly here. The bird feeder is a flurry of activity with juncos here in number, forecasting winter. In some areas they are called snowbirds. A hairy woodpecker is monopolizing the feeder while being challenged by white-breasted nuthatches and chickadees. A pair of cardinals comes and goes, and white-crowned and white-throated sparrows add to the interest.

Recently I came upon a Friday, January 10, 1908, copy of *The Onaway Inter-Lake,* edited by J. Edward McMullen and published weekly, "The Official Newspaper of Onaway and Presque Isle County." It cost one dollar per year, in advance, and entered in the post office of Onaway as second class matter. Here are some excerpts from this issue:

> "Advertised Letters. List of letters remaining uncalled for at the Onaway Post Office, January 10, 1908: Bert Burden, Peter Gota, Miss Gertie Gota, Wm. Doane, Joe Francis, G. F. Glover, Mrs. Charles Hanchick, Anton Kanjorski, Clarence Landen, Albert Marshall, Ward Mather, Chester Nye, Walter

Nichol, Mrs. Emma Phillips, E. J. Tomkins, Carl Zarske, Meredith Franklin. While calling for the above, please ask for advertised mail. I. J. Barnett, P.M."

"A Long Runaway. Monday evening as Velma Quance was out for a sleigh ride, accompanied by her friend, Amelia Plower, one of the thrills broke and, hitting the horse, caused it to run away. Starting at Lounds on Sixth Street, it came out on Main Street, making a beeline west. As it passed through the business portion, Velma stood up like a charioteer in a mad race, holding to the line as best she could, and succeeded in passing several teams without a scratch. On and on the horse went at a furious speed and was not stopped until the handle factory at Tower was reached. It was a ride that neither girl cared about repeating and fortunately nothing more serious than sore hands and arms resulted to the little driver."

From the Riverbank
April 19, 1995

The Card Game of Spitzer

Our family has always played cards, and Spitzer and Contract Rummy are all-time favorites.

Spitzer became a part of my vocabulary when I was about sixteen years old. My brother Homer was teaching at the Town Hall School in Moltke and roomed and boarded with the Adolph Karsten family, quite close to the school. What an undertaking for a young man just turned 18! There were 55 students ranging from kindergarteners through grade eight, and five or six of the beginners spoke only German. It was natural that the teacher should learn the card game of choice in the Moltke community, and of course that was Spitzer.

Homer began to teach the rest of the family the game, and it became our adopted family game, along with Pedro, Canasta, 500, and a few variations of rummy. But Spitzer became the favorite family card game because of the challenging aspects of the game. Whenever the family was together with enough players, the card deck was stripped to 32 cards and Spitzer was on the table. The method of banging the cards briskly on the table was called "Moltke Style," and players that dawdled and played slowly were admonished to play "Moltke Style."

I had a chance to sit in on a hand or two of Spitzer at the senior supper last week and really enjoyed it. You can usually find Glen and Arlene Cryderman playing with Al and Zenie Jarvis. Ted Skinner and Orrin Freier keep the cribbage board busy, with others keeping track of the counting. Many solitaire games help wile away the time before the meals. I must get there earlier and perhaps we can organize another game of Spitzer.

* * *

I always like to speculate when the ice will break up on Black Lake. The Roberts family history has been closely attached to the lake since the very early 1880s, and it was handed down to me that the 19th of April was the average date to expect the ice to go out. With a warmer than usual winter, I guessed that the 10th might be break-up date, and I kept a close watch from several locations. Bob Marshall, from his vantage point on the Bluffs, confirms that actually the 12th of April should go down in the journal as official for this year. So be it! This should mean somewhat earlier sucker and mullet runs. What we really need to get real smelt runs is some rains. The forecasts keep promising rain, but as I look out at the Black River from my front porch, I see more exposed banks than I can remember.

From the Riverbank
November 17, 1993

When the Game Changes

Basketball, hunting, and winter activities change over the years, and we must change with them.

"Thursday, January 12, 1933, Onaway beats Alpena 14-9. Bob Pregitzer was high point man with six points. Others playing: Wheeler, Cassibo, Robinson, Jackson, Aikens and Huila." Ed gleaned this gem from the State Library, which has many years of *The Onaway News* on microfilm. Ed suggested that the low score indicates a remarkable defense, but what is your guess?

I played basketball in junior high and high school at about this time, and it surely was a defensive game. I played stationary guard, and if a guard dared to go beyond the center line, the coach promptly pulled him from the game. It was okay for the running guard to mix it up in the forecourt. This definitely kept the scores low. Then Pellston put a team on the basketball court that was billed the "point-a-minute team." That figured out to the astronomically high score of 32 points per game and even higher. Yes, the game was dramatically changed.

Another game that has seen lots of change is deer hunting. Our hunting uniform was simple and cheap. We bought a yard of red chambray material from Gumm's Department Store, cut it into strips, and sewed it onto our overalls and jackets. Not much sitting for us. We had to keep moving just to stay warm! If we had a warm cap with earflaps, we were all set. Blinds with piles of apples, carrots, corn, and sugar beets were unheard of. Often we could track a large buck track for a few hours, jumping it as it became careless and possibly get a killing shot. Today following a deer is the best way to put the deer in the sights of some other hunter. Just a lot of hunters out there…and another game has changed.

* * *

"Let's eat out for lunch!" Sounded great to me, as I'm now chief cook and bottle washer, so together we packed the picnic basket. Simple fare: hot dogs to roast on an outdoor fire, carrots, apples, bananas, plus a thermos of hot water for tea and coffee. I kept thinking, where? And suddenly it came to me. Yes, a spot along Canada Creek where we went cross-country skiing with Jim and Phyllis Snody many, many years ago.

Some apprehensions. Could we remember the exact spot? Would the old two-track road still be passable after all these years? Last Thursday was a grand sunny day, and as we homed in on our special spot, our spirits lifted. It was just as we had left it 20 years ago. I quickly had a nice fire going in a secure fire ring of stones. (It helps to bring your own kindling and wood). Our tailgate lunch was so very nice, and then we walked the trails where we used to ski. We will always remember this outing with pleasure. Who said picnics were only for summer!

* * *

I'll be "stalking my deer" in the doctor offices of Burns Clinic on opening day and will bring my "dear" (Idamae) home with me. Come to think of it, there have been lots and lots of opening days that I didn't bring my deer home.

Not on the Road
December 9, 1992

The Car in the Garage

It was our winter tradition to head south for several months. Here is a story from a year we stayed at home.

By this date last year, Idamae and I had traveled 2,464 miles down the road toward warmer places. So where are we today? Right at home in Onaway! My navigator has turned in her road atlas and maps, and she has declared that this is the winter we stay home and enjoy stoking the stove and shoveling snow. I can accept that, and am looking forward to ice fishing and some cross-country skiing. However, the camper is in the GO readiness mode. If Old Man winter delivers a knockout blow, and my navigator starts hunting up the road atlas and maps, I'll be ready.

* * *

The odometer of our 1984 car said too many miles. Although I thought it was good for at least another season, there was a campaign for a newer car. "Okay, I'll have Virgil look it over if you will agree to his decision."

The inspection day came, and the recommendation was that I should probably start looking for a newer car. I was prepared to go home and announce that a newer car was in our future. When I went to pay Virgil, he said, "You don't owe me anything. Your wife came in and paid me to tell you it was time to find another car."

* * *

Woodsheds come in many sizes and shapes, and all of them have slightly different smells. As a boy, beech and maple were the only woods considered right for our kitchen range; kindling woods were tamarack and cedar. What a good aroma! Of course, poplar and elm added to the blend. As I smell the mix of woods in my woodshed right now, the smells take me way back into my memories.

Sixty-five years ago, stove-length wood was a winter cash crop for farmers. My dad bought stove wood for Hankey Milling Co. (the elevator). It had to be piled, and mostly it was piled on top of snow. As summer approached and the snow melted, it fell over. We kids were paid 10 cents a cord to re-pile it. Before we could collect, my dad would lean on the new pile. If it withstood this test, we got our money. If it fell down (and often it did), we learned to pile it right the next time! To a ten-year-old, making 30 cents on Saturday really was "the good old times."

From the Riverbank
January 15, 1999

Making the Most of Winter

Some years we escape for a good portion of the winter, but when we are here, we make the most of it through a variety of activities. Cross-country skiing is one of them.

Our children have been asking when we are going to leave for warmer places, and the answer, until ten days ago, had been, "Why leave such lovely weather?" When we were greeted with 16 inches of snow and forecasts for a steady diet of more of the same with very low temperatures to boot, it didn't take long to dig out our Elderhostel catalogs.

We knew it was late, but were able to locate a neat sounding program at Camp Thunderbird entitled "The Wild Life of Wildlife—Fly Away!—Where Do All the Birds Go?—Starlight, Star Bright: Florida Campground Astronomy." Sounded good for starters. We located another program on Galveston Island entitled, "Island Sampler: Birds, Biology, Bays Beaches, Buccaneers, and Bull!" Now to fill in the time between these Elderhostel programs. A few days stopover in New Orleans to enjoy pre-Mardi Gras, some birding along the Mexican border, and hopefully the worst of winter will be over.

Actually birding has been good right here. We spotted one bald eagle on Monday and two on Tuesday, a pileated woodpecker last Friday, and far more starlings than in recent winters. Coyotes, too, are out and about during the day, and a neighbor saw one running on the river.

* * *

I have yet to get down the "thin slats" and try out some of the cross country trails. A friend gave me an ancient pair of skis that have a single strap, requiring you to jam the toe of your boot under it. They are big, heavy, and cumbersome. I would break trail with them, since those old skis were so wide that it was very easy for the rest of the gang to follow. I still have them somewhere but probably don't have strength to maneuver them. The new groomed trails really are great, so I must get those newer thin slats down and clean and wax them (yes, I'm of the olden crew that still tries to match the waxes to the type of snow).

I'm reminded of an encounter on cross-country skis many years ago. I was leading my family members and friends on a trail when three or four snowmobilers approached us head on. They weren't traveling fast, but it became quite obvious that they automatically assumed that the trail was theirs and cross country skiers would step aside and give them the assumed right of way. However, it didn't work that way. They slowed, turned off the trail, and we proceeded in a straight line. I think they were as surprised as I was.

I'm happy to know that trails are groomed for both snowmobiles and skiers, and each group respects each other. Now if I can just find the right layers of clothing to keep me warm and still able to move....

From the Riverbank
May 10, 2002

The Onaway Historical Museum

Onaway history and memorabilia are housed at the Onaway Historical Museum located in the old courthouse.

I had a pleasant visit with Norman Foster, a collector from Grand Blanc. Norm graduated from Onaway High School in 1953 and moved to the Flint area to find work. One of his hobbies has been collecting memorabilia, especially about Onaway. Other things he collects include early radios, telegraph equipment, and early Daisy BB guns.

Norm brought the following items to me to be taken to the Onaway Historical Museum: a wooden steering wheel made in Onaway, an autograph book with many Onaway entries including my parents, Onaway related postcards, and a commemorative coin distributed for Onaway's 50th birthday. I will take these items to Harriett Lyon, who will see that they are added into the museum collections. This is how a local museum grows.

PART THREE

On The Road

This travel outfit symbolized our love of adventure. Idamae and I traveled the north, south, east, and west of the U.S. and Canada during 1977-1992, meeting America and her hospitable people.

Almost every November we set out to become nomads, escaping the rigors of northern Michigan winters. Favorite destinations were the Gulf Shores, Louisiana, the Brownsville area of Texas and California. We encountered many Michigan "snowbirds" on our journeys, some from amazingly close to Onaway. We also enjoyed visits with family and friends. We would return home to Onaway in March or April after having traveled 10,000 to 12,000 miles. The articles here cover travels from 1989 to 1992.

Florence and I still travel, but as age creeps onward, "softer" accommodations and more a sedate existence suit our plans.

Cliff and Idamae in southern Arizona with saguaro cactus

On the Road with Cliff and Idamae Roberts
December 31, 1989

Louisiana and Texas in 1989

Since we traveled the same or similar routes for many winters, Idamae and I enjoyed returning to favorite campsites. We learned to weather the cold there just as we know how to in Michigan.

A lull in the early morning rain prompted a hurried take down and departure from Dulac, Louisiana. Morgan City builds and outfits offshore drilling rigs, and it was here we stopped at McDonald's for breakfast. French flowed freely, as a busload of senior citizens joined us. They came from the Cajun lowland parish (we would say "county") of Lafourche and were en route to an annual religious pilgrimage. Fun people and language no barrier.

Sugar cane is the major crop here, and I stopped to talk with some workers. "Follow those tractors loaded with cane, and you'll see the sugar factory," they offered. Such a sight; dozens of trucks and tractors lined up for weighing and unloading. I got many pictures. All the drivers wanted their pictures taken. Then Trent Downing, plant manager, came out and offered me the full tour. This is big business. The raw sugar (light brown) and molasses-like syrup are loaded into barges and sent via the rivers to New Orleans for final processing.

We drove the Atchafalaya levee road to Fausse Point State Park, arriving there at dusk in a cold drizzle. We made our first concession to the cold weather and rented a large cabin ($50 for the first night, second night free). We decided we needed a couple of days in spacious housing. Weather was still a problem when we left; muddy roads and more rain. We planned to stop at Sea Rim State Park near Port Arthur, Texas. One look at the barren, wind-swept area in coastal marsh grass was enough. No thanks!

On another 75 miles to "camp" at Holiday Inn in Baytown, Texas. It was so cold in our second floor room that we had to move to a first floor room to get out of the wind and be warm. An early start and a resolve to "run for it" took us south to Goose Island State Park. We saw thousands of snow geese flying and eating in fields of harvested milo. Also saw hundreds of sandhill cranes. At a gas stop in Port Lavaca, someone asked, "What part of Michigan?" Would you believe it, Mark not only knew where Onaway was but owns hunting land near the old Schell cobblestone house on Berranger Road. He had hunted there this season and now lives in Port Lavaca. Small world.

We arrived at Goose Island to warm sunshine, and we set up on site 123, exactly where we had camped in 1984. It was cold that night, but no difficulties. Someone said fish were biting, so I bundled up with everything I could find plus my insulated coveralls. Caught a nice redfish and some too small to keep. Good eating.

We bought jogging pants to supplement our night clothing, and they really helped. Remember, we are in a tent-camper, and the temperature went down to 12 degrees! Our electric heater and our gas furnace both worked well, but it still wasn't any too warm. On top of that, our LP gas tank ran dry about 4 a.m. As long as we stayed in bed, we were warm.

I went back to fish, but the low water and temperatures had caused a massive die-off. Mullet, redfish, and drum and sea trout were dead and dying. (Illegal to pick them up, so they are wasted.) Our supper on Christmas Eve was at Pizza Hut. So much to take home. Guess what we ate for Christmas breakfast and dinner? Pizza!

We played tape recordings of past Christmases—1953, 1954, and 1974—to bridge the gap and bring fun and laughter into our camper. One Christmas card hangs above our door, a work of love and art. Thanks, Peggy.

On the Road with Cliff and Idamae Roberts
January 3, 1990

A Cajun Wedding

We enjoyed real Cajun hospitality during our time along the Gulf Shore.

The last Gulf Shore activity, a Christmas musical celebration "Of His Kingdom—There Shall Be No End" at 1st Baptist Church. A beautiful message in music, a real baby in the manger, and super refreshments and warm hospitality afterward.

Driving one day, we stopped to visit some men trying to keep warm around a big campfire. A Good Club from Mobile on their annual Christmas outing. They thought I was the local fire marshal. Southern hospitality—it's here. They invited us to their dinner and program.

It's good to be on the road again. I'm sure we are travelers. The call of what is ahead is much stronger than the magnet to stay.

Bayou Segnette State Park, 20 miles southeast New Orleans. Lots of birds, sunny days, and cold nights. Our gas furnace and an electric heater kept us warm. Drove to the very tip of the Mississippi River delta. Off-shore oil and gas wells, big business—workers out to work on the platforms by helicopter, seven days out, seven days home. Tasted Satsuma oranges grown on the delta—sweet, like tangerines.

Next move was south west to Dulac, Louisiana, to try to locate our Cajun welder friend Niles and his buddies. Found his sister Annie instead and talked with Niles by phone. While eating lunch at Annie's Restaurant, we were invited to her sister's real Cajun wedding on Saturday and to set up our camper across the street in her father's backyard.

While Idamae napped, I visited with a shrimper who suggested I stop at D'Luke's shrimp processing plant to see how it was done. Royal treatment by David Luke (owner of D'Luke Seafood) and his staff. After a tour of the shrimp processing, I left with a calendar, some frozen shrimp, and memories of real Louisiana folk.

As we readied for the wedding, sirens began wailing! Just Santa Claus on a fire engine escorted by the police. The wedding was at 1st Baptist Church of Houma, 17 miles north of Dulac. Truly a multiracial group of about 175 people. The reception was in the church fellowship hall, with such good Cajun food: gumbo, jambalaya, rice (lots), and a ham and navy bean and rice dish selection, as each cook tried to out-do the others.

So good being invited into this family sharing, freely and easily done with two strangers. True Cajun hospitality. Annie and eight sisters and two brothers attended out of 14 children. Shot two rolls of film of reception activities for Annie to share with her family.

Will stay a few more days in Louisiana before moving out to southern Texas. No idea where we'll be for Christmas, but "Merry Christmas" to all our good friends and neighbors.

On the Road with Cliff and Idamae Roberts
March 10, 1991

Arizona, Texas, Oklahoma, and Arkansas in 1991

Visiting Twin Wells Indian School years after the time when Idamae and I served as volunteers there for extended periods during the years 1977 to 1980 was a special treat of our West winter travels.

Verde Valley near Sedona, Arizona, was the best of camping, but comes the time to go. Sure, we had heard that Flagstaff had lots of snow, but that was for people who had skis on top of their cars. Big surprise as we topped 7,000 feet; we were the ones who might be skiing! Possibly three inches of snow, and the plows were out. This was winter again. How beautiful, but we had enough of beautiful earlier in southern California. As soon as we reached I-40 and headed east, all was well.

Brief visit at Twin Wells Indian School, where we got a status report of current activities. Carmelita Little was a tenth grader at Twin Wells Indian School and was in my homeroom in 1977. Carmelita graduated from Winslow High School and a nursing school in Kansas and now is chief lab technician at Winslow Indian Hospital. Great to see these Navajo youth take their place in the world. Tail winds of 35 to 40 mph hurried us all the way to Albuquerque this day and pushed us to Amarillo, Texas, the next day. We were in Central time zone and definitely closer to Onaway.

Good stop with Idamae's brother Wilbur Lorentz and his wife Judy in Oklahoma City. Judy really knows how to cook; good thing our visit was for only a weekend. Wilbur, ill from kidney failure, keeps alive by dialysis four times daily. He loves to play cribbage, and we played almost non-stop for three days.

We had our warmest weather of the winter in Oklahoma City, and from sun up Saturday until sun down Sunday, the leaves opened as if by magic. High temperatures and recent rains helped. We were kept glued to the "tube" Sunday p.m., as tornado alerts were watched. Nothing too close to our location.

We left Oklahoma City and swung back into Texas quite close to the storms in Dallas-Fort Worth area. Sarah and Ernie Hosier, friends from Twin Wells Indian School days, are both in Regency Nursing Home in Clarksville, TX, and share the same room. Ernie turned 90 years old on March 2.

Our next stop was Texarkana, Arkansas. Won't set up the camper anymore; relying on Tom Bodett to steer us to "camping" sites. Flooding and rain damage all across northeast Texas and into Arkansas. We crossed all of Arkansas today, from Texarkana to Memphis, Tennessee. So many of the rivers out of their banks, and for once it felt good to be following Joe. This is our last *On the Road* for this winter season. Stops at Cincinnati and Holland to see kids and grandkids, and then home!

If you watch national weather reports, you know that over two months in Texas meant lots of rain, but we have thoroughly enjoyed our winter odyssey and met so many wonderful people as well. We'll see you soon in Onaway, and thanks for letting Idamae and me into your homes via the *Onaway Outlook*.

On the Road with Cliff and Idamae Roberts
December 19, 1991

Florida in 1991

What makes a campsite good? We had plenty of opportunities to evaluate them!

Monday was travel day, and we took a backwoods route most of the day. Piney woods gave way to cotton farming, and then we noticed a different type of harvester and specialized wagons. We were in peanut country near Malone and Campbellton, Florida, just a ways south of Dothan, Georgia, the peanut capital of the U.S.

Needing to increase our pace, we dropped south to I-10 and traded scenic beauty for miles. We also traded for confusion, as we negotiated a "goat's trail" thru Pensacola. Rule One: Always follow the road your navigator selects.

It was amazing what interesting places we saw this way. However, once we saw the intercostals bridges at Perdido Bay, it was clear sailing to our Gulf Shores destination. Site #239 seemed like home, as we'd spent a week or two on this site in 1989 and in 1990. We turned our camper so our windows look out on a beautiful lake with no other campers in view. Lakeside sites are $12 per day, $60 per week, and $175 per month. We opt for the long stay, not knowing whether we could actually stick out 30 days in one place. We were immediately contested for our site by ants, but a series of stratagems out-foxed them, and we are in sole possession.

How do you rate a campground? If it is just for an overnight, we can accept most any conditions, but for a week or longer, we look for the following:

1. Clean toilets and shower
2. Wide sites, not too close to other campers
3. Walking trails and paved streets within the park

4. Reasonably close to shopping and churches

5. Always unobstructed morning or afternoon sun

Quite an order, yet we find many that score well on all counts. Gulf Shores is one of the best. We also tend to find friendly people there as well.

Shopping at Wal-Mart in Foley, Alabama (about a dozen miles from our camper), we met Roger and Ruth McFall. They had come in the same day as we arrived. They are about a quarter of a mile from us. Lots of Michigan people have found this place, but not so many this season. I asked at the park office, and they said it's called recession! Only half as many here as at this date last year.

A racket in the bushes interrupted my reading, and a sharp-shinned hawk captured a robin and made off with its meal. Reminds me of a tobacco ad of fifty years ago: "Nature in the raw is seldom mild."

Part of this week has been occupied writing and addressing our Xmas cards. Easy duty, sitting outside in full sun. Kind of blots out the northern Michigan winter scene.

Next week we check and double-check the area maps for interesting places to visit. We will share some of our wanderings after the holiday season.

On the Road with Cliff and Idamae Roberts
January 6, 1992

Louisiana and Texas in 1992

Another Christmas season enjoyed on the road.

Our truck has a compass mounted on the dash, and it really helps in navigating. At first it pointed SE, but now it has been pointing West. Actually the compass is very valuable while traveling through cities. Our altimeter has been pretty flat after leaving the Appalachians, but later on it will be interesting to watch.

We have two packages of maps labeled "ahead" and "behind." There is a constant shift of contents as we are out.

Louisiana might have been named "Swampiana." So much swampland, with Cypress groves and bayous everywhere. Our destination in Louisiana was Villa Platte (flat ground). The Cajun influence there is very strong. Many greetings of welcome in French. We revisited Pig Stand restaurant, but it had gone downhill to a 4th rate place.

Chicot (chee-co) State Park was our destination, a very pleasant place to stop. We were blessed with very good weather. Cooked and ate outside and enjoyed campfires for several days.

Snow geese by the thousands go north each morning to feed in rice fields, returning by dusk to find suitable overnight spots. Bored with camp life, we made a 100-mile clockwise circle, seeing rural Louisiana—sugarcane, cotton, soybeans, rice, and plantations of pine. Recession is a reality here! A young man said, "No matter how poor your job is, hang onto it!" Many road signs said, "Drive Carefully Substandard Roads." They really were!

As we left Louisiana and headed into Texas, we thought we might see flood damage, but the Sabine River was quiet and well-mannered. Not so the Trinity! We will really check at the bad places next week as we move from Galveston, crossing the San Jacinto, Brazos, and the Colorado Rivers.

Our first encounter with Thousand Trails Preserves was at Lake Conroe, Texas, north of Houston. A 90-day perk from the Fleetwood camper purchase. A very clean, pleasant place to camp. A patriotic program presented Saturday evening was a flag-waving rouser. We all shared in singing the great songs of American freedom. We seem to be in senior citizen groups wherever we go!

Some of last summer's bounty of canned salmon became tasty salmon patties, mostly cooked outside as they stink up the camper—but oh, so good! I also whipped up a meal of pork jambalaya. It was so very hot with Cajun spices. I'll bring the recipe home.

We are 50 miles north of Houston, with remarkably warm weather. Don't believe all those TV weather reports of nothing but rain in Texas. As we leave tomorrow, we will check into our second Thousand Trails Preserve on Galveston Island. The compass will point SW, as the coastal bend of Texas lures us sunward.

Our Christmas cards received remind us of our good friends from Onaway and all over the country. When the camper is closed up for the night, the TV tuned to our favorite programs, the warmth of the heater, a game of rummy or cribbage, or a good book, one could be Anywhere USA!

On the Road with Cliff and Idamae Roberts
January 27, 1992

Texas Times Again

Is it any wonder we spent many a Michigan winter in Texas?

A Michigan license plate "RAPTOR" needed investigation. We met Jack and Nancy Waldron, who live on the west side of Burt Lake. We shared birding and camping information. They travel in a monster motor home pulling a Jeep.

We shared a nice time together with Bill and Ginger Francis from Virginia, both near 80 years old. Their license plate "GUD TERN" alerted us to their interest in birding. We met again at Bentsen Rio Grande Park in Mission, Texas.

The Good Samaritans of Rockport sponsored a stage play, "The Drunkard," to raise money for their ministry to the needy. They hoped to raise $2500. The "winter Texans" all came, and they raised $4000. Seven churches participating comprise the Good Samaritans.

The Leepers camped across from us. They live in north central Indiana. We enjoyed their campfire, which was made possible because they bring their own wood with them from home. "Gathering Firewood Prohibited" is a rule in the state park.

We enjoyed a good potluck at The United Methodist Church and then a slide program on Bolivian missionary work. Shared in another slide show, "Black Creek Colonial Farm," in the Toronto area. This church goes all out to meet the needs of winter Texans.

This was "Laundromat and Wash Everything Day." I got out of the way! After that, we were ready to get on the road again. Two weeks seems a long time to stay put. At 5 a.m. both of us were awake, so we "pulled stakes" and left Rockport in the semi-fog. Pre-dawn breakfast stop in Alice was a great start for this day. A roadside stop later to smell the early flowers and stretch our legs. The valley looked very inviting, with fields of aloe vera, carrots, cabbages, broccoli, onions, and red peppers. Harvesting was in process on many farms. Fewer citrus orchards; most did not replant after the devastating freezes of '84 and '89.

We set up in Bentsen Rio Grande State Park and found our friends from Argosy, Indiana, only three campsites away. A summer-like day with the temperature at 70 degrees. Now, to get lots more like it.

Our furnace failed to fire one cool morning. Called Fleetwood in California and then the warranty service in Corpus Christi. I hated to take the camper so far, so I started checking wiring connections and got lucky—just a poor electrical connection.

We were wakened exactly at 7 a.m. by our "smart TV" with "Good Morning, I'm Harry Smith. and I'm Paula Zahn."

Springtime comes after lots of warm rain, so it must be springtime here! Actually, it is. Peepers singing in water puddles, grass very green, leaves popping on some trees, and the birds really singing. Groups of birders can be seen each day. Sometimes there are more birders than birds!

Otto and Hilda Marquardt invited us to join them for church and then brunch at Shoney's. They are quite well and active in their Texas Tropic Star Mobile Park. So good to visit with them. They will join us for lunch at our camper on Thursday. If your ears burn, you'll know we are sharing the good days they spent with you in Onaway.

On the Road with Cliff and Idamae Roberts
Date Unknown

Arizona and California

As we traveled south during the cold winter months of Michigan, at times we encountered the West's own version of a rough winter.

Kind of hated to leave Pima County Park, next to the Desert Museum just west of Tucson. This is Sonoran Desert at its best. Bright, cool mornings, daytime clear and warm; just enough evening clouds to produce beautiful sunsets, and then the singing of coyotes at night. I tried to get good recordings of the coyotes at night, but not as good as I wished.

AJO (AH'Ho"), AZ. Lunch at the Copper Kettle; appropriate, as this whole town seems to be owned by Phelps-Dodge, the Copper King of Southern Arizona. Stopped at Wellton, Arizona, where the closeness to other campers protected us from strong winds. A gas stop at a BLM (Bureau of Land Management) site found five or six hundred RVs camped haphazardly on the barren desert. No water or electricity or sewage disposal! But since it is free, lots of people stop.

Yuma area just great farming—alfalfa hay stacked in rows 12 to 16 feet high, about 10 feet wide, and 100 feet long—miles of it. They probably get five good cuttings and use the old-time, small, squared bales. Asparagus, lettuce, and carrots being harvested—"stoop labor at work."

EL CENTRO, CA. A grocery stop, then on to Ocotillo, well-named for the dominant desert plant. Saw many gorgeous rainbows as we went north through Anzio Borrego State Park.

We weren't prepared for Stagecoach Trail Park, perched on a mountain side, wild winds buffeting us. Gave up searching for a campsite and drove 17 miles to Julian to get our mail. Thanks, Marcella! Fifteen miles up a narrow mountain road that peaked at 4,200 feet. Some of the rain looked flat. We were whipped plenty, and next-door neighbors offered the sanctuary of their RV if we felt threatened by the 30 to 40 mph winds during the night. "Our light is on. Come in at any time." We survived the first night of wind and rain but had to pull out sleeping bags, as all electricity in the camp went out at 4 a.m.

The price of getting letters is to write, so this was special correspondence day, which meant paying bills also. A pancake breakfast at the lodge was doubly sweet as we shared experiences with couples from Oregon and Colorado. During a siesta, a monstrous wind burst almost toppled us. We immediately made ready to take down the camper in wind and rain. We planned to sleep in the truck, but at 5 p.m. we left and tried to find a better place.

Rain turned to snow at 3,300 feet and two inches on the ground at Julian. Gassed up and asked for directions from Julian, through El Cajon, to Jamul (I was informed it was HOOL'ian, El Kahon, and Ham'ool.) Stopped at Ramona Valley Inn and left for "Ham'ool" early Sunday morning.

Pio Pico is a Big Thousand Trails Preserve with about 300 sites. Campsites G & H (where we stopped) have no sewers, so they give you a sign, "Honey Wagon," to be put out on your scheduled day. This service is free, as sites across the road have sewers. RVs are constantly moving to the sewered sites as openings occur. We are not in this shuffle, as our "Porta-Potti" is easily managed.

The Thousand Trails and NACO people are also nomads, so maximum stay is two weeks. A special problem was caused by big flooding in the Los Angeles area and the closing of many campgrounds. President's Day long weekend brought in lots of children and grandchildren to visit with grandparents. Sitting outside writing this is a luxury after so many cold, windy, and rainy days.

Thursday we visit old-time friends from Twin Wells Indian School days. Dorothy and Max Greene are only about 50 miles from our camp. Hope I can report on continued good weather from Southern California.

On the Road with Cliff and Idamae Roberts
March 3, 1992

California Heading East

Our travels took us to many out-of-the-way places, but we were able to make some amazing connections with family and friends along the way.

Jim's Avocado Ranch needs extra hands, but not enough for full-time workers. Mexican nationals usually do this work, but Montayo, a Guatamalan, showed up on his motorcycle. He carries a green card and is a good worker. He earns $5.65 per hour. He is rapidly learning English, and just this week he found housing in Escondido for his wife and three children. While we were there, I had the experience of grafting new stock onto avocado trees. Now all I have to do is wait four years and go back to California to pick the crop. We said fond farewells to Jim and Hazel and were loaded down with tangerines, oranges, limes, and avocados. We made the U-turn, and the compass now points eastwardly.

Funny thing happened as we stopped at Blythe on the California-Arizona border. The RV camp we selected was almost under the I-10 bridge crossing the Colorado River. Remember the old song, "The railroad runs through the middle of the house"? Well, this was similar, only it was trucks this time! We had a mostly sleepless night. No intruders, but the intrusion of lots of road noises caused us to be much more careful in selecting camping spots!

Cactus is very closely associated with altitude, and our altimeter verifies this: saguaro about 2,800 feet to 3,200 feet, cholla and ocotillo below saguaro, and so on. The manzanita tree is always at 4,500 feet, and the Creosote bush grows where nothing else can make it.

The climb from Congress, Arizona, to Prescott was beautiful, challenging, and exciting. Prescott was also a lunch and grocery stop. Pretty city. Our truck worked as we peaked near 6,000 feet. The truck needed servicing, so we stopped at Oil Can Henry's. Fifteen minutes later, we were on our way with oil and filter change, lube, and all systems checked.

The scenery at Verde Valley is spectacular. We set up overlooking the river and were greeted by 75° weather even though the altitude was 2,300 feet. Dropped to 22° overnight but quickly back to 65° by noon. We called Mary and John Hinson to give them directions to find us. Some talk of rain.

Today we visited Sedona. There aren't words enough to describe the beauty of the stone formations. The usual tourist traps, fudge shops, "artsy" places, but we shunned these to visit the Chapel of the Holy Cross.

I have been winning too many rummy games, so we switched to Cribbage. Idamae beats me repeatedly! Oh, for a way to play two-handed Spitzer.

Finally washed the truck and camper. California is still under strict water use regulations. People reduced their use of water so much that their water billings increased! Doesn't seem fair.

Big snow forecast for Flagstaff, and skiers will rejoice. Don't think it will affect us, but possibly some rain. We are watching Onaway weather more closely now.

Mary Hinson had a story to share when they arrived to spend the day with us. Anna Munger Dunn, Mesa, read in "On the Road" that the Hinsons were going to visit us in Cottonwood, Arizona. So she looked up Hinson's phone number and asked Mary to share her greetings with us. Idamae and Anna grew up as neighbors. A great idea, and a big thanks, Anna! *The Onaway Outlook* really does get the job done!

On the Road with Cliff and Idamae Roberts
Date Unknown

California Again

How interesting for us backwoods Michiganders to be driving on California urban freeways!

Yes, the weather continues to be great at Pio Pico. We are in a small valley about 25 miles southeast of San Diego. Our next-door neighbor, a career Navy man, has an elaborate model train set under the front of his big fifth wheel motor home. A much larger scale than "O gauge" trains, and it attracts lots of attention with flashing lights and life-like sounds. John retires next month to become a full-timer; his rig will be his home.

California traffic is something else. We planned our visit with Dorothy and Max Greene, who live in Vista. We left camp after "go-to-work traffic" and started back before the "go-home-rat race." It was still quite hairy, and I'm so glad for our quiet roads in Northern Michigan and especially Onaway.

We had no idea they could perch so many homes and condos on the mountainsides and tops. The Greene's live in a beautiful home overlooking a small amphitheater. Close enough to the ocean so that air-conditioning is not required. Glad to see them, but we are all getting older, and it seems unlikely their health will allow them to do much traveling in the future.

We experienced a small earthquake just at dawn on the 18th. It was quite close (about 20 miles), at El Cajon, but it was small—3.30 on the Richter scale. No damage or injuries. Still, the people are jumpy, always wondering if this is the start of "the big one."

Our feed sack is open, and many birds come to our table. Crows, house finches, white-crowned sparrows, black phoebes, towhees, and even bluebirds. These lovely, feathered friends constantly cheer us with their beauty and songs, also saying, "Spring is here!" A special treat was to see hundreds of western grebes on Otay Lakes. Saw a large Olympic training site under construction. Will try to find out more about it.

It is laughable to see the variety of dogs. Some say dogs resemble their owners, and that may be true. I'm sure we have recognized dogs from some other locations. The miniature collie twins, for example. We saw them first in Alabama and then Mission, Texas; later near Houston, and now they show up in Pio Pico. These dogs travel more than a lot of people.

Just yesterday I talked to a lady with a pet goat on a leash. "It doesn't shed hair or have fleas. I like it." A miniature Chinese pig gets lots of attention. I'm sure companionship plays a big part, and some think of their dog as a security guard.

It's difficult to find a town or shopping center (as we think of them) in these southern California mountains. We haven't seen a Wal-Mart or K-Mart or an honest-to-goodness mall since leaving Yuma. I make sure gas tanks are full at all times. People must drive unrealistic distances to their jobs. Give us the simple life!

Our visit with Jim and Hazel Evans in Valley Center was special! Jim and I went to college at Ypsilanti, and both of us were in the Industrial Arts program. We belonged to the same fraternity, and our kids are of like ages. Hazel and Idamae organized picnics with other friends. Jim and Hazel, retired from the L.A. area, having taught there for years. They moved to Ventura County and planted a 15-acre avocado and orange grove. They are still doing the work and enjoying good health. How great to pick your citrus for breakfast.

Hillsides are ablaze with California poppies. I suppose our dandelion fields would be considered very beautiful by Westerners. I'm getting anxious to see them. As a kid, dandelions in bloom meant suckers running in the Black. Still hope to be home in time to catch a few.

PART FOUR
Other Writings

Family is everything! Pictured here is Ann, Bruce, Paul, our dog Jet, and Dale c. 1958 on the steps of our family home at 117 Ripley Ave. in Alpena. It was a really nice house with upstairs bedrooms for our growing family, close enough for children to walk to school, great yard and garden area, and only a few blocks from the Thunder Bay River, which provided us with great fishing for all the children and me too. All of our children graduated from Alpena Public Schools. But when the flock "flew the coop" as all children eventually do, Idamae and I gravitated to Onaway to purchase a delightful home on the banks of the Black River. After Idamae's death, Florence Webster and I married and moved to our present home on Black Lake.

The writings in this section span from 1973 to the present. They include personal writings, tidbits on family life, newspaper articles including "From the Lakeshore," and writings by others.

Feb 28, 2008

A Brief Look at Our Children

I didn't journal much during the years we were raising our children, so here is a look back at our family then and extended family now.

Idamae and I had four children, in four different locations, and decided no more moves! Our children were born as follows:

1. Bruce Alan (February 10, 1945) at Burns Clinic (Petoskey, Michigan), ten days after I returned home from having been discharged from stateside Army Air Force service.
2. Ann Elizabeth (March 3, 1948) at University of Michigan Hospital while we were living at Willow Run Village (housing for discharged veterans attending college under the GI bill).
3. Paul Edward (February 1, 1951) at Escanaba Hospital while we were living in Escanaba.
4. Dale Michael (March 27, 1957) at Alpena General Hospital while we were living in Alpena.

Bruce was a charming youngster, and we looked for a daughter. Ann arrived three years later and added such joy. Paul was born while living in Escanaba, and he became our hunter and fisherman. Dale was born six years later to complete a car full.

Alpena became our home in 1952 when I joined the Alpena Public Schools, and I served in many capacities there until retirement in 1977. In Alpena we rented a home at 1006 Ford Street and then bought our 117 Ripley Street home. We finally built a substantial home at 2970 Ontario in 1962, mostly by myself with lots of help from Bruce, a senior in Alpena High School.

The family soon scattered. Marriages added spouses, children grandchildren, and great grandchildren. Our nest is empty.

After graduating from University of Michigan, Bruce went to the Peace Corps in the Philippines, married, and moved to Cincinnati. His children are Erika and Adam, Joel, and Eve. Bruce and his wife Karen now live in Colorado. Ann married a fine local boy, Dan Glawe, and they made their home in Alpena. Ann's children are Wendy, Cindy, and Jenny. Paul attended Michigan Tech at Houghton and furthered his education by sailing on the Great Lakes freighters and becoming a journeyman plumber. Paul is living in the Alpena area. Dale graduated from Hope College in Holland, Michigan, married Jeanine, and made Holland home until a recent move to Temperance, Michigan. His children are John and Mark.

Florence's children David, Steven, and Diane were born in Flint. Dave lives on Black Lake, Steven lives on Black River near Cheboygan, and Diane lives near Elk Rapids. David's children are Suzanne, Eric, and Katie. Suzanne and her husband Ryan Betker live in Wisconsin near Oshkosh. Eric is in Minneapolis. Katie lives near Grand Rapids. Steven's child is Lauren. Lauren is attending university in Portland, Oregon. Diane's children are Cody Nichols and Trevor Thompson. Cody is in Wilmington, North Carolina.

At the time of publication, we have seventeen great grandchildren. Child of Dale's son John is Jack. John is currently attending Northwestern University near Chicago.

Children of Ann's daughter Wendy and John Braeutigam are Laura Ann, Daniel, and Luke. They are living in Lansing. Children of daughter Cindy and David Bell are Kristian, Joshua, Alec, and Ann. They are living in Alpena. Children of daughter Jenny and Chris Gallo are Richard, John, Sophie, and Christopher. They live in Lansing.

Children of Bruce's daughter Erika and Chris Sammond are Tony, Noah, and Chloe. They are living near Cincinnati. Children of daughter Eve and David Wilkerson are Bryce and Brianna. They live in Indianapolis. Son Adam and his wife Melissa live in Cincinnati. Son Joel Bozman lives in West Carrollton, Ohio.

Journal Entry
June 17, 1967

Leaving for the Peace Corps

Our eldest son Bruce went camping with the family one last time before his two-year term with the Peace Corps in the Philippines began. His example of service inspired Idamae and me to serve as volunteers a few years later at Twin Wells Indian School.

We were camping with Dale, Paul, and Bruce in Canada north of Lake Superior when it was time for Bruce to leave for Peace Corps training in San Jose, California. It was a dismal night as we drove to a nondescript, small, backwoods train station in Marathon, Canada. His duffel bag was packed, and we waited quietly until the train approached. Parting was brief—a few tearful goodbyes, knowing that we would not be together again for more than thirty months.

We drove silently a few miles to our deserted campsite. Then Dale, our ten-year-old son, said, "We are not much on ceremony in this family, are we?" He was right. It was a proud day that a son who had just graduated from University of Michigan and had offers of promising employment with Procter & Gamble was off to a far part of our world to help make life better for others. As we crawled into our sleeping bags that night, we all experienced sadness as well as being proud of having Bruce leaving to share his knowledge and expertise with others.

Letters from Twin Wells Indian School

Shortly after my retirement in 1977, Idamae and I joined the volunteer staff of Twin Wells Indian School, a boarding school for Native Americans located in Sun Valley, Arizona. I worked as a teacher, and Idamae worked in the kitchen and the library and office. We were there during the entire 1977-78 school year, March through the end of the school year in 1979, and again in March through the end of the school year in 1980. Following are excerpts from some of Idamae's letters sent to our family.

August 30, 1977. School started this morning. Most of the 200 registered children are here, 30 more than last year. The ten kindergarten children are so cute—so innocent—so scared. Some of them do not speak English. The dorm parents are to be admired, as their job seems to me to be the most work and worry.

We've been here four days, and it seems like much longer, as we are so busy. I know we will grow in Christian love this year as we spend our time in the beautiful atmosphere of love we feel among the entire staff. The staff is about 65 percent young people—dedicated Christians—full of love, care, and concern, and fun to be with. Two couples are with the Christian Service Corps out of Washington, D.C., here on a 2-year term. They pay their own way through sponsors back home.

Cliff went to his first class this morning with "butterflies" in his tummy. He has one eighth grade math class, four shop classes (and no shop), and the 10th grade home room with which he spends the first half hour each day in a prepared Bible study. He has been helping on the construction of a new dorm, badly needed, which will hopefully be finished in November. He really enjoys that. He has seven tenth graders.

I am working in the kitchen, one of a 2-woman shift—don't laugh! I try not to. I mostly follow orders. They are really short of kitchen help, good or bad! I may get to the library mornings when I'm on the afternoon shift and afternoons when I'm on the morning shift, but right now I'm mending sheets, blankets, towels, and children's clothes.

We have a sewing machine in our apartment for a while, until the Home Ec wants it.

Our apartment is two large, carpeted rooms with bath, adequately furnished with a stove, sink-top over a small refrigerator and a 1 ft. by 2 ft. counter top. It's all we need, as we eat in the dining room and enjoy the fellowship.

You can see for miles in all directions here. We have been walking a mile or so morning and/or evening—seeing new plants, flowers, mountains, mesas, lizards, beetles, and cactus. The land around the school is open range—horses and cows (a dozen or so each) graze on it. Some nights the horses come up by the apartments to eat our grass. They are not afraid of us when we meet them on walks, but we do not touch them. It is, of course, not good pasture, so it will not feed large herds. Twin Wells could fence them out, but the rancher doesn't have to fence them in, except from the highway with cattle guards, as it is open range.

The wind blows almost all day, bringing some sand with it. The weather is much like our northern Michigan weather in August—80 degree days but cool nights. Snow is not uncommon in winter. We are at 5,000 ft.

The drinking water is alkaline—Cliff has nearly given up coffee—it tastes so terrible. I'm not minding it too badly. Some of the staff go to a laundromat in Holbrook and get water, which is good. We may try it.

As soon as the Indian parents drive away, their children are treated for head lice. Not all children have them. They also are showered and clothes changed. They do not object nor feel badly about it. They don't like lice either. Bless those dorm parents.

The children may go home any weekend their parents can come and get them after October 1, with the stipulation that all children are back for Monday courses. They all go home at one time for one weekend each month. All staff is free for that weekend, from Friday night until Sunday night, except dorm parents must be around Sunday noon for returning kids.

Indian parents are proud to have their children at Twin Wells, so there is a waiting list of kids, some who are now in Bureau of Indian Affairs schools, which do not have the Christian caring of Twin Wells.

* * *

September 2, 1977. We're here, it's for real, and we are very happy and so busy that the days seem like two instead of one, and that's good. Just received the staff list this morning; 52 on staff including employees. There are 13 volunteers from Michigan, others from AL, VA, PA, CA, IN, IL, MN, WA, NE, OH, CN, TX, CO, GA, and OR. One couple will be coming soon from the Netherlands for six months. Everyone is so nice to know and work with.

Cliff is teaching health to 7-10th graders, shop, and has the 10th grade homeroom. Yesterday as he entered the 6-10th grade building, he heard one of the boys say, "Here comes Oral Roberts." He gets along with them very well. They like to tease.

I'm cooking—with a lot help. We work one week from 1 p.m. to 6:45 p.m. and the next from 5:30 a.m. to 1 p.m. When I'm not cooking, I will be helping in the library and helping mend sheets, quilts, and kids' clothes. I'm really enjoying it. Also gets me acquainted with some of the kids as they help with dishes, serve, and clean up in the dining room. Just like all kids everywhere, they do their job, but not because they enjoy it.

It's a beautiful picture to walk into the chapel and see all-black heads. They fill the chapel—staff sits on the sides. They are happy children, have fun together on the playground, but they fight too. There are little red wagons for the small dorms, and the little ones have such fun with them. They cry, litter, tease, and dislike vegetables, chores, and studying. One first grader was homesick yesterday and was crying, "Mama, Mama." I nearly cried too as we tried to comfort her, but I saw her at suppertime, and she was okay.

It takes five or more sponsors at $15 a month to keep each child here plus other donations of food, clothing, books, supplies, and money. I feel everyone on staff tries to use all supplies carefully.

The parents are so proud to have their children at Twin Wells. One thing they are learning because they have two Indian ministers on the reservation is that they can be Christians and still be Navajo. They are so proud of being Navajo; in fact, they are the largest Indian tribe around here. The tribes do not always get along well together.

Most parents drive a pick-up truck. They can have used clothing from the store room if there are things the children need. They can also buy some of the older quilts for 25 cents each, which they are glad to get. There is a trend now for the Indians to buy house trailers—large ones—to live in instead of hogans. Of course, they cannot hook up the plumbing, what with no water. One little girl said they keep clothes in the bath tub and use the toilet for a chair.

We just praise the Lord for this opportunity. It's a service of love, but we are reaping rewards beyond our imagination.

* * *

September 7, 1977. We are both busier than I've ever been! This week is 5:30 a.m. to 1 p.m., and I'm really tired when I'm done—too tired to mend quilts. I've been trying to do some much needed extra cleaning in the kitchen and so haven't even had a coffee break. The two head cooks are 73 years old, so they can do their cooking but no extra scrubbing, which the place needs.

Cliff and I sat at the kindergarten and first grade tables the last two nights to give the dorm parents a break. Buttering rolls for 16 kids, making sure they eat all their food, wiping noses—it was fun. They are so sweet.

It really takes a lot of work to keep a place like this going. The count is 185, but two less today, as two 7th grade boys ran away last night. The staff is sure they went home, but there is no phone on reservation where they live.

It's 96 degrees here today—was 60 degrees last night. The dry heat is not too bad. I work 13 days and then I'm off from Saturday 1 p.m. to Monday 1 p.m. We may not go sightseeing this weekend.

Cliff is really enjoying teaching now that he has health instead of math. He has one boy for 10th grade shop, a very nice boy. I'm sure Cliff will learn much from Julius about Indians, this land, etc. This boy's older brother is a minister.

This week each child was measured, as the Navajo nation gives each child two complete sets of clothing for the school year. Some of the money comes from the sale of wood, but I don't know about the rest yet.

Holbrook is a mixture of Mexican, black, and Indian, along with a few whites. We are getting water at the Laundromat now, and it's good.

* * *

<u>September 26, 1977</u>. We made mutton stew one day last week from a whole butchered sheep. The kids were really pleased, as they are used to it and have to eat so many of our foods....

A week ago Sunday after I got out of work at 1 p.m., we took our supper and hiked for an hour to look at some funny-looking black, round, low hills near Holbrook. On our way we saw tons of petrified trees, some lying as whole trees; others looked like wood chips lying all around. It was really fascinating. Picked up some samples, as many as Cliff could carry in the backpack. Also found some pottery shards. We were gone about four hours just walking from the school.

At 2:30 this morning I woke up to cows eating grass outside our window. That's what it's like out on the open range. We heard coyotes one night last week up on the hill near here.

* * *

<u>October 7, 1977</u>. Each day our lives are enriched as we work with these children. I'm sure this would be true of any group of children in this particular situation. We praise and thank God for this privilege.

A week ago Saturday the menu called for hamburger soup, fry bread, and peaches. Five seventh grade girls came to make the fry bread. They start making it when they are six years old. You mix flour, baking powder, salt, dry milk if you wish, and water, and then knead it until it looks like bread dough. Each girl takes a piece of dough a little bigger than a golf ball and pulls it and pats it and stretches it over the backs of both hands. Then it is fried in about an inch of hot Crisco, turning once. It puffs up and is really delicious.

A week ago Saturday Cliff led a group of 30 adults 75 miles southwest to groves of pinon pines with loads of pine nuts. Such fun to find something to scrounge from nature. We put two old blankets on the ground, Cliff shook the tree, and out of the cones they came. They are such tiny morsels to eat, but oh, so good. Many of the kids here have them in their pockets and are chewing on them whenever they can.

This week we have a Navajo pastor and his wife here for a 3-day revival. Two of their children go to Twin Wells. The children are all so good in chapel. They love to sing, and sing many Bible verses they know. We have the old-fashioned hymn books, so we sing "In the Garden," "Trust and Obey," and "The Lily of the Valley."

I'm hooked on these wide open spaces, beautiful sunsets, thunderstorms you can see happening miles away, a sky full of stars, and being able to hang clothes out at 3 p.m. and still get them dry in an hour or two.

* * *

<u>October 27, 1977</u>. No rain since October 4, and that means sunny days. It has been 34 degrees at 6 a.m. most of this week, but it gets up to 70 degrees by 10 a.m. I can see why Northerners come to Arizona!

Cliff's shop is going well now, and the boys are pleased. He is also doing lots of picture printing in the dark room for sponsor pictures plus taking and printing others around the school. The kids all like to see themselves in pictures.

This weekend all the kids go home. We plan to take five kids home to Ramah, New Mexico (south of Gallup about 135 miles). We will camp nearby, do some sight-seeing until Sunday, then bring them back to school. One girl, Fern Pokagon, is a girl our church circle in Onaway sponsored for two years. Her dad is a minister at a reservation church. He is a Potawatomi Indian from near Petoskey.

Last Saturday afternoon six of us went north to the Hopi reservation to First and Second Mesa. Hopi Indians lived there on a mesa about 500 feet high and 100 feet wide in stone pueblos inhabited since the 1500s. You can walk around the village. Some sell pottery, Kachina dolls, and food from their homes. At first Cliff was reluctant to walk around; said it was like somebody walking around our house, but the people we were with convinced him it was okay.

Sunday afternoon a family who had three boys here—one a 10th grader who Cliff was very close to (transferred to Winslow High) invited us to their place. We were not in their house, but they and their relatives were riding steers and horses, bucking, to get ready for the rodeo. Cliff took lots of pictures. They talked Navajo to each other. We wished we had had our tape recorder. Then they took Cliff to see a cave in a nearby mountain about two miles away.

The Gift of a Poem for Christmas

The following is a poem written for Idamae in 1983 at Christmas.

Our Christmas gifts, spread over the years,
Have been practical, sturdy, and sometimes brought tears.
How difficult it was, finding gifts that were "right,"
How little the means, to make Christmas bright.

Toys for the kids, mostly made in the shop,
Helped stretch Christmas dollars, by Mom and Pop.
Doll clothing, wood trains, scarves and toy guns,
Made Christmas days merry, and full of fun.

As our kids got bigger, and job more secure,
Gifts changed in size, numbers, and in allure.
Less time for Santa's workshop, Mrs. Santa too,
Store bought things (and bigger) just had to do.

And before we knew it, our kids went "skidoo,"
Each had their own place, and their own things to do.
But each Christmas season, our family would meet,
To share common love, some gifts, what a treat!

All year has been Christmas, as we bought our own gifts,
And we found worldly things, couldn't give us the "lift."
We are blessed with children, grandchildren, things from above,
So what's left to give? Just all of my love!

Merry Christmas, Sweetheart.

An Anniversary Letter to Idamae

October 11, 1942, was our wedding day, Idamae received this letter from me in 1973 on our anniversary.

Dearest Idamae,

Happy anniversary! It's been such a short time; it's been such a long time; it's been such a wonderful time together. Your love has been the light of my life, making all other things pale and insignificant by comparison. I am so fortunate that you are you and you are mine.

The years together have been good. Some struggle, some small adversities, but mostly just wonderful events. We have been blessed with children and now the extra blessings of grandchildren.

Our work situations have always left us time for our family and each other, and for this we can be especially happy. Our picnics, drives, walks, trips together as a family have caused us to know and understand and love each of us more. Looking back on 31 years of living together, I can only say again, "I love you, and may the future continue the richness of blessings that have been ours."

With all my love forever,

Cliff

Journal Entry
March 1988

Bone Marrow Rebirth of Ann and the Family

Daughter Ann suffered many years with cancer before her complete healing in 1988.

Ann was really ill this time. Her cancer that had been put into remission for five years by chemotherapy had returned. University of Michigan Hospital had determined that it was non-Hodgkin's lymphoma but were unable to come up with a cure. However, Harper Grace Hospital in Detroit had been doing work in this field and was on the cutting edge of this disease.

A bone marrow transplant from a person with matching bone marrow was the only answer. Three siblings were potential donors. Bruce and Dale had their bone marrow tested, but there was no match. Paul might be the answer, but he had been in Florida for several years, and his present whereabouts were unknown to us. With a diligent search by Ann's husband Dan, including help from some friends of Paul, he was located. Paul agreed to the expensive testing in Florida to see if his bone marrow matched. Eureka!

Paul then traveled to Harper Grace in Detroit. Bone marrow was extracted from his lumbar region. When Ann was prepared, an IV was used to transfer the bone marrow into her system. Her Mom and I were in the room for the bone marrow transplant.

Ann saw some improvement but soon needed special platelet transfusions from matching blood. Paul and I drove to the Michigan Red Cross Center in Detroit, where blood from Paul was centrifuged to remove the needed elements to be transfused to Ann. I was with Paul for the whole procedure. The platelets were introduced to Ann by IV, and within hours Ann showed improvement!

Paul and I returned to the Red Cross Center about a week later, and the procedure was repeated. This time Ann's improvement was remarkable and was the start of real recovery. Praise the Lord!

A few weeks of recuperation in the hospital, with daughter Cindy in constant care of Ann, made the difference. The trip home to join the rest of her family was an answer to many prayers.

"I was reborn on my 40th birthday," Ann said. She put this thank you to Paul in the *Alpena News*:

> *To Paul—*
> Thank you for the gift of Life.
> Your Loving Sister
> *Ann*

From the Riverbank
March 9, 1994

Reflections on Idamae's Homegoing

After a brave struggle with pancreatic cancer, Idamae Roberts passed from this life to the next on January 23, 1994.

Families need to gather for important celebrations: weddings, birthdays, graduations, reunions, and funerals. Weddings are my favorite celebration, but all have their place. Our family and friends gathered recently for the "homegoing" of Idamae, my wife of 52 years.

How could this lovely creature of God have touched so many people? As this phase of life changes, I can only thank you for your kind thoughts and faithful prayers.

Idamae and I didn't share our planned January picnic in the out-of-doors, but the seeds and bulbs, so tenderly cared for during the later summer and fall, will burst out in renewed beauty as another spring and summer approaches. There are already signs from the riverbank that the joy and beauty of spring can't be far away.

April 1999

The Gift of Grandparents

The following was written by granddaughter Eve (Bozman) Wilkerson during her senior year of high school for a writing contest. She knew Idamae for only a few years, but the love she received from her grandparents was life changing. In the end, it's really all about family, isn't it?

I don't remember the first time I met my new grandmother or the last time I saw her. She was a godly woman who lived in the sticks of northern Michigan. She and her husband lived in a small cottage heated by a wood stove that looked out on Black River. The name of the river had always interested me, and in my naive youth I thought that the water must be black. I never got to figure that out, since it was always frozen and blanketed with snow upon my annual arrival.

I would arrive agitated after the ten-hour drive with my family of six. All this agitation would dissolve when I saw Grandma smile at me walking through the door. Speaking more to herself that to anyone else she would say, "There's my little china doll." This always put a smile on my face, as I would stare at her and wonder what exactly she meant by that. Regardless of what it meant, it always made me feel loved.

There were things about her that just stuck out from everyone else. At the end of a meal she always refused desert and reached for an apple. She seemed as content as I was with my cookie. For her funeral she had asked her husband to wear the same suit that he wore the night he asked her to marry him. Now he was not the type of man that this was easy for him to do, but he did it. He looked almost ridiculous, and no one understood why he was wearing that old tie that no longer reached his middle until he explained with tears in his eyes that he was doing it for his wife Idamae. His precious wife, he said, had wanted this event to be a celebration, not a funeral. She wanted everyone to know that she was finally going home. I saw Grandpa smile as he looked at his yellow shirt and snug jacket. I saw him as a better person because she loved him.

I sat in the pew of that small church on the day of Grandma's celebration looking around at her family and friends and not truly understanding what was going on. I looked at all the people that she had loved who were now missing her. They all had a look in their eyes that spoke to me. They were saying to me that they were better people because of knowing Idamae Roberts.

In Grandpa's speech that day he mentioned some of the things that made Grandma so special. One of them was that daily she would pray for every person in her family and many of her friends. He had found a very extensive list in her Bible of everyone that she prayed for. Somehow I knew that next to my name on that list, in parentheses, were the words "my little china doll."

To this day when I think of my grandmother I have a burning desire to simply be a better person. Many times I have recalled and admired my grandmother's pure heart. It was the heart, I realized, of a woman who knew Jesus. She is with Him now, just as He was with her in her life.

Grandma's life taught me the most important law of life: faith. She taught me that faith is more that a verbal commitment, more than believing, more than a relationship with God. It takes a life of action. When it is over, we will hear His welcoming voice whisper our names and then, just for me, something like "my little china doll."

My Journal
May 5, 1994

Sentimental Journey—Second Homegoing

The cardboard box with Idamae's ashes was delivered to Chagnon's Funeral Home on February 4, and there it remained for about six weeks. When the postman brought a package to my door, I knew what it was, and I chose not to unwrap it. It stayed unopened on the floor of the spare bedroom for another several weeks. I tried to ignore it, but Friday, May 5, was the day I began following the wishes Idamae and I had chosen to care for the remains.

I cut open the package with a small, plastic knife with a bit of trepidation. The contents resembled some stony-like material and unidentifiable black particles, but it was mostly small bone fragments.

Collectively we had chosen to have the ashes scattered among the places we both enjoyed some of our sweetest memories. Camping spots and places we both loved and treasured, places where we had picked berries, rivers and streams we had canoed, places we had picked mushrooms.

A slight rain was in the air (sometimes heavy) on the day I began the journey to return Idamae's ashes to the places of her choice. I didn't know just how it would go, and if I could really do the thing we both had agreed should be done. I thought first of the small cassette recorder (didn't work) and then the desktop recorder (it also didn't work), so I took a camera to document the places I would scatter the ashes (I'm trying desperately not to say the word *remains*).

First stop at Crockett Rapids. Slow start. The camera didn't work. Then I remembered the Konica back of the truck seat. A word of prayer and why "we" were here, and my routine got underway. I could do it!

Next stops (in order) were Barber bridge, Main Stream bridge, mushroom patch, triple culverts on Pigeon River, Clark bridge, McMasters bridge, Milligan bridge, Erratt bridge, and finally our Black River swimming hole out front of our house.

As I drove from spot to spot on this journey, the "good times rolled" in my mind, and I chuckled, laughed, and cried a bit. "How great Thou art, Lord, to have made it possible for Idamae and I to spend so many years together, and to especially enjoy the Pigeon River country!"

These journals will help me re-live our joys when the mind fails to remember; and our children and grandchildren may one day read some of the accounts and recognize bits and pieces of a truly great love story. Amen and amen!

From the Riverbank
March 3, 1998

New Paths

For a while after Idamae's homegoing, life seemed, as poet Robert Frost has said, "... too much like a pathless wood." Then Florence Webster and I were married in 1996 and moved to Black Lake in 2002. Together we have discovered new paths, including Elderhostel programs, great escapes in the winter, and also tremendous learning experiences.

Florence and I left home for Hawaii on the 27th of February and missed all the very wild snow blizzards. We flew from Traverse City to Minneapolis and then non-stop to Honolulu for eight and a half hours airborne. On to Hilo on The Big Island to rent a car and start our tour going clockwise. We found some super good Bed & Breakfast places and leisurely enjoyed the 70 degree night temperatures and clear skies with mid-80 degree temperatures during the daytime. Back to Honolulu to join 38 other Elderhostel members. We were housed in the Pagoda Hotel, and our classes were in the penthouse of the hotel.

The Hawaii Pacific University staff challenged us with astronomy and history, including the Arizona Memorial, Pacific Art Forms, etc. We then took a short flight to Maui for an additional week of study and field trips, including a whale watching trip on the Pacific Whale Foundation Whale observation boat. After some volcanic history was a trip to Mt. Haleakala to observe one of the more recent active volcano sites.

Three weeks away from home was enough, and we returned to the land of the deep snow and big rains! My river depth marker had registered five feet above summer normal in front of our house. The exotic birds of Hawaii cannot compare to the robin, cardinal, junco, and redpolls, and we assure you it is great to be home.

From the Lakeshore
April 25, 2003

Signs of Spring at the Lake

The break-up of the ice on Black Lake is the most dramatic sign of spring, but the songs and calls of birds are the first welcome indicators.

That haunting call of a loon during the night was proof positive that spring has truly arrived. Most of the ice was gone from Black Lake, providing a landing spot and the long space needed for loons to take off. There was no answer to the wail of the lone loon, but surely a resounding return voice will bring these wild things together.

Early morning songs of goldfinches and redwing blackbirds, the kingfisher chattering, the killdeer's plaintive calling, and the "kree, kree" call of the high-flying sandhill cranes snap my head skyward to spot them. The cranes can be heard for two or three miles. Yes, spring is really present, officially or not!

April 21 or 22 was ice-out day on Black Lake. High piles of ice pushed up along the shore from Harbor Light all the way to Taylor Canal. No reported damage to cottages, but it was very close to some buildings, in some cases only a foot or two away. One of my early predictions was for a May 1 break-up (this date also shared by Bob Bonner), but I'm happy to have been wrong.

From the Lakeshore
July 25, 2003

Reflections

This piece is the tale of a bird having to deal with its reflection.

A red-breasted cuckoo has made life interesting around our house this spring. Now if there were such a bird, I would have alerted a number of Audubon Society folks, but actually it was a "cuckoo" robin redbreast.

A banging on a window that went on and on was driving us batty! An adult robin kept hitting the window with its breast, making a lot of noise, and as often as 20 times per minute. What to do? I called some birders. They were aware of cardinals being a nuisance with this behavior but not robins. I found some pictures of owls and hawks and scotch taped them on the exact place on the window that was being attacked, but this didn't change anything. In fact, at times the robin brought worms as it approached the window. This certainly was a "cuckoo."

After a number of weeks, it dawned on me that this was a double-glazed window, and the bird was seeing the reflection of itself. At first it was trying to frighten the image, and later the mothering instinct caused it to bring worms to feed its reflected image. The ways of wild things are strange, but much to our relief, the robin got on with normal pursuits, and the window banging ceased.

This is the time of the year that adult birds bring their young to feeders to introduce them to "the easy life." We were fortunate enough to have three adult tufted titmice visit us during the winter to get their share of black sunflower seeds, but then we didn't see them for about two months. They showed up about three weeks ago with four youngsters. The same has been true of rose-breasted grosbeaks and purple finches as well as chipping sparrows.

From the Lakeshore
September 17, 2003

Fall at the Lake

Our birdfeeders here at Black Lake give us daily delights, as does looking out at the lake from our deck out back.

Selective feeding of birds is a common practice. The kind of food and the amount it costs us cause us to limit the kind and amount of food that is put out. If we were trying to feed the smartest and possibly one of the most beautiful birds, we would put lots of sunflower seeds on an unobstructed flat surface and welcome the blue jays. But watching the supply of food being gobbled up and carried away seems to go against our feeling of fair play. Special feeders that limit the amount and kind of food is one answer. Feeders with varying size openings limit the size of birds who want that particular type of food.

I had a bluebird nest that became empty when the baby birds flew away with the parent birds. An enterprising pair of starlings enlarged the size of the opening and decided to call this birdhouse their new home. I chose not to have a starling family (hoping the bluebirds would return and raise yet another clutch). So I used the old mending material, plastic wood, to reduce the size of the entrance hole. It worked! The would-be renters tried to re-enter the nesting hole, but they could no longer fit, and plastic wood was so hard they could not enlarge the opening as they had done before. It was amusing to watch them as they tried to push their bodies into the hole. I'm sure they thought, "We fit before. Could we have put on this much weight?" After repeated tries, they gave up and sought another hole to rent.

As I look out over Black Lake, very few boats can be seen, and most docks and boat hoists have been removed. Schools are in session, families visit only occasionally, and the summer renters are no longer here. It doesn't seem too long ago that the dock and hoists were put out. One item that we will not miss is the incessant noise of personal watercraft. The sunrise and moon rise are more beautiful this year due to the addition of more smoke haze from forest fires in the West.

The trees are starting to show some color changes. Most of the early color changes are due to trees being in a stressed situation—too dry, damaged, etc. The many types of grasses are at the peak of their beauty. Even the spotted knapweed as well as the purple loosestrife, both considered weeds, add much to our outdoor scene.

From the Lakeshore
April 15, 2004

Zebra Mussels on Black Lake

Besides Florence's annual reporting of ice out dates for Black Lake, she also collects data on zebra mussels.

The long, elusive spring has finally arrived. My nephew, Harold Schmidt, clued me in on the fact that suckers have started to run at Muskrat Landing on Mullet Lake. Robins are plentiful, and numerous other spring birds are here. So get out that fishing gear and enjoy. Oh yes, new fishing licenses are needed.

Black Lake ice is so close to being all gone that I'll make the prediction that the lake will be free of ice by this weekend. There has been very little shore damage. We took pictures at a number of places, and it has been gentle.

Dr. Ken Stewart, Professor of Biological Science, State University of New York, made his annual call to Florence for her report on Black Lake "ice out" (he has called her for 12-15 years for freeze over and ice out dates). He also asked if she could collect specimens of zebra mussel shells at a number of locations along the shores of Black Lake, so now she has the title of Zebra Mussel Detective. There is a strong similarity between the Finger Lakes in Dr. Stewart's vicinity, so this information might add to the comparisons.

So, if you see Flo hunting the shoreline with me tagging along, we haven't lost anything. We are just collecting zebra mussel shells.

Alaska Letter

The letter that follows was written to Kaye Sloan, a childhood friend of daughter Ann, during our 1997 Alaska journey, my fifth to that state.

Dear Kaye,

After we left you, we traveled towards Denali without a clue as to where we would stop for the night. A $140 per night motel didn't attract us, so on to Healy for a nice enough motel in the $40 range. Up early to meet our scheduled bus and start the Denali experience. A fantastic day, without even a trace of clouds. We opted for the six-hour trip, and it was long enough. Such grand scenery and enough wild animals to make it interesting. Many, many caribou, some moose, a few eagles, and a grizzly. Got plenty of pictures and some videos.

On to Fairbanks to "Alaskan Experience" B & B. This couple from Onaway and nearby Millersburg had a "fantabulus" place. We had our pick of three rooms (more like suites) that boggled the mind. Snacks and all the good breakfast things, but no one came up with a better true Alaskan breakfast than you shared with us!

We went on the Sternwheeler Discovery III trip on the Chena and the Tanana Rivers, enjoying especially riverbank visits with a River Fish Camp and a great visit with Susan Butcher and family. On the return, we got off at the Athabascan Village and had a chance to learn from natives about their culture and crafts. A great adventure. Visited the museum but found it decidedly inferior to the Anchorage Museum (or the Wasilla Village). We shared a very good halibut meal prepared by Mary and Dan McClean.

Off towards Valdez and looks at the Pipeline on the way. Too far for one day, so when we got to Glennallen, we got on the phone and found Carol's B & B. We were leaving our phone numbers everywhere we stopped and kept in constant touch with Linda, Florence's daughter-in-law, who is a nurse. The reports were not good on the condition of Florence's 97-year-old mom, Dorothy Smith.

Stopped at Worthington Glacier and walked up to the ice field. Fun and lots of pics. While at Carol's B & B, made reservations at Angie's B&B. She was packing up and leaving that very week for Washington! Got lucky and booked a night with Gussie's. This is among the very best! The family owns a Christian bookstore in Valdez.

Took the Prince William Sound tour on the LU-LU-Belle, and it was a fantastic choice. Lots of sea otter, out to rocky crags to be close up to puffins and seals. Then to the face of the Columbia Glacier and back near Valdez. We spent 40 minutes in very close proximity to Delta Dawn (a major salmon netting boat). Such fun, and some pulleys broke, but they were able to pull in their 30- or 40-ton catch of silvers. Next day was the Pipe-Line Terminal tour, and a good one.

News from home this morning caused us to call Northwest Airlines and change our departure. Our trip became a 10-day one instead of the 22 days we'd planned. Back to Carol's in Glennallen and heading for Anchorage Sunday morning. Our flight was for 7:25 p.m. Sunday, and a very good trip home. Long layover in Detroit, but got home to Onaway about noon on Monday. Flo's mother was very ill, and we reached home for a farewell visit, as she died a day and a half later.

Volunteering for Hospice

The following article by staff writer Derek Hatfield appeared in The Onaway Outlook *on Friday, November 3, 2000. It was accompanied by a photo of Florence and me.*

The hospice program caters to patients in the terminal stages of illness, and anyone who has ever cared for a terminal family member knows that this is a difficult thing to go through. Volunteers like Cliff and Florence Roberts of the Onaway area try to make things a little easier.

"We have been involved since spring of 1996," said Cliff. "My wife of 52 years had been a hospice patient, and I was her primary caregiver. So I decided to go through the training and volunteer. Florence and I were not married at that time. We met in the same training course and had similar goals. We basically go visit people when the caregiver needs to get out for a while."

"Or when they just want someone there," added Florence. "That is usually toward the end. Plus, there are usually other little things to do. Go to the grocery store, light household duties, and sometimes taking care of young children. There is one elderly lady who goes to the hospice house and bakes cookies to make sure the cookie jar is always full."

The primary purpose of the program is to make patients comfortable and keep them as pain-free as possible.

"Though we have been through the training, we don't involve ourselves in medical matters," said Cliff. "We do the visits. Sometimes we go together, and occasionally I drive to the hospice house and do little chores such as changing light bulbs and following the vacuum around."

"When (volunteer coordinator) Sally Hardy calls us to make a visit out of our area, sometimes as far as Wolverine, she will give us background on the patient so we aren't going in cold."

"The sad thing is that most people don't bring patients into the program until the end, when they should be brought in earlier to gain the full benefit of the program. It is more than just nurses; there are also social workers available. It helps the rest of the family as much as the patient."

"The most rewarding thing is sitting with the patient and family in an area where I know parents and children so that they know someone else is there."

"This is the kind of work that can be done by people of any age. I celebrated my 82nd birthday, and I think it is a great way to get out in the community and meet people."

Flash from the Past: Cliff and Florence Roberts

The following, submitted by Historian Kaye Porter, appeared in a November 2006 Onaway United Methodist church newsletter mailing.

From Cliff: The Roberts family was among the earliest pioneers of the Onaway area, having come from Canada in the 1860 era. They homesteaded on Stoney Creek about two miles west of M-211 near the Cheboygan County line. Their Onaway home was near the elevator, and I was the sixth of their seven children.

I attended Sunday school at the United Methodist Church. I have memories of the old church and Mr. Shackson as Sunday school superintendent. I recall Mrs. Harmon was my fourth grade Sunday school teacher. Mr. Karr made my Sunday school very special. My older brothers were in a class of about 20 taught by Rev. Clifford.

Sunday school was held in the Epworth League room. I recall my father getting up in the sanctuary when Sunday school kids were anxious for their classes to begin or when the pastor was running overtime. Dad was a stickler for Sunday school to start on time.

I had the distinction of being married twice in this church. Idamae Lorentz and I were married by Pastor Fred Hart in 1942. Idamae died after 52 years of married life. Florence Webster and I were married by Rev. John Hamilton in 1996.

After 34 years of sharing my time in educational pursuits in a number of schools, I retired from Alpena Public Schools in 1977 and returned to the Onaway area. During my working years I kept in touch with activities of the Onaway United Methodist Church while my parents were still active. My mother, Maybell, was still making pies for church activities well into her 90s. She had flowers from her yard on the altar way back. My dad brought them over before the service. This continued even after my dad's death.

There are few offices and jobs in the church that I have not fulfilled. Choir has always been a joy, and currently both Florence and I are choir members.

* * *

From Florence: I, Florence (Webster) Roberts, and family moved to Black Lake from Flint in 1961. Rev. Dorraine Snogren was pastor. The new church had just been built, and a lot of interior work was done by volunteer church members. My husband Lloyd and I helped with painting and with other interior jobs that needed to be done. At the time our two sons (David and Steven) and daughter (Diane) were very young.

Donna Buckley was the first Onaway UMC member I met. We met in the laundromat, and a finer friend I couldn't have. We later worked together as teacher aides for 17 years at the Onaway Elementary School.

I became a member of the W.S.C.S. (new United Methodist Women) in the early 60s and served as secretary several times and on the nominations committee. It's a fine bunch of ladies.

We attended Sociables (monthly) right from the beginning, probably in the early 70s when Rev. Charles Ball was our pastor. We enjoyed it very much. We had progressive meals once a year, hobo dress-up and potluck meals one month, a hayride in the fall with a cookout, and ate at the B & C Restaurant buffet one month a year, where probably 45-50 attended from both churches then.

I have served on various committees over the years—pastor parish, nominations, and administrative board trustee. I joined the church choir in the mid-80s and enjoy it very much. I also have been in our Christmas Community Choir for 20 years or more and always look forward to it, seeing old friends and meeting new people.

Cliff Roberts and I married in December 1996 and have been blessed with ten years together. Cliff and I feel very blessed to have found love twice in our lives, where many never find it once! The church family is a very special part of our lives, and many of our best friends are right here.

PART FIVE

Photo History

Onaway Courthouse
(Photo courtesy of: Ken Huisjen)

Onaway is located at the western edge of Presque Isle County at the junction of M-68 and M-33. This area was first settled in the 1880's by Thomas Shaw and Merritt Chandler. Chandler was the first to plat the land, naming the town after an Indian maiden, Onaway. This town grew during 1903. Shortly after that, Merritt built a courthouse on the western edge of own intending to attract the county government to locate there. It never appened. Now the building contains the local historical society, the district Presque Isle Library, and Onaway city offices.
(http://www.infomi.com/city/onaway/)

Cliff Roberts in
Army Air Force uniform

Cliff and Idamae 1943

Idamae, Bruce, Cliff, and Ann Roberts in front of
Oscar Roberts' Onaway homestead 1949

Clifford R. Roberts 243

Oscar Roberts' Onaway homestead

Maybell Roberts with all seven children
(Back row left to right: Cliff, Homer, Earl)
(Front row left to right: Arden, Ruth, Maybell, Vera, Clarence)

Hankey Milling Co. elevator, Onaway, Michigan, c. 1950

Maybell and Oscar Roberts
in homestead dining room

Oscar Roberts

Clifford R. Roberts 245

Onaway Train Depot and Freight House c. 1920

First Train to arrive in Onaway c. 1899
D & M #17 steam engine

D & M diesel #481 RS-2, Alpena Train Depot c. 1950

(Photos from D & M Railway Historical Society, www.dm-hs.org)

246 *Stories From The Riverbank*

Bruce, Paul, Dale, and Ann, 117 Ripley Ave., Alpena

Paul and Dale with salmon 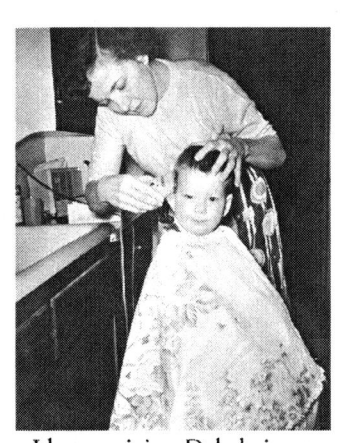   Idamae giving Dale haircut

Bruce and Ann at Roberts' Onaway homestead c. 1949

Clifford R. Roberts 247

Cliff with 20-lb. northern pike
1938

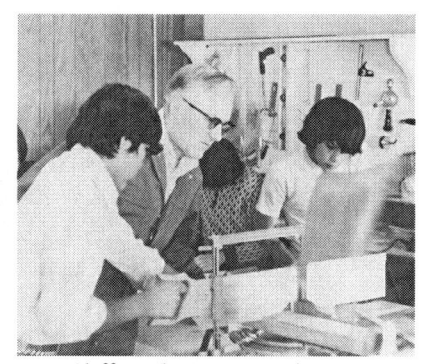

Cliff teaching Navajo boys
woodworking at Twin Wells
Indian School

Cliff with nice catch of trout at
Roberts' homestead with elevator
in background

Cliff and Paul

Cliff and Florence, married December 1996

"Sally Hardie presents Senior King and Queen Cliff and Florence Roberts of Black Lake with their trophies after they were announced as winners. Cliff is a 50-year resident of the area and was one of the earliest Hospice volunteers in Cheboygan."

(2006 newspaper caption regarding Cheboygan County Fair)

About the Author

Clifford Ronald Roberts was born October 16, 1918, in Onaway, Michigan. He was the sixth of seven children born to Oscar and Maybell (Fairman) Roberts. He graduated from Onaway High School in 1937. After graduation, he attended Presque Isle County Normal in Onaway, a one-year preparation yielding a two-year certificate for teaching in country schools. He taught for two years in Presque Isle County's one-room schools.

Clifford married Idamae Lorentz (born July 16, 1924) on October 11, 1942. On July 6, 1943 he enlisted in the Army Air Force and served as a cryptographer. He was discharged from the Army in 1945. He completed his bachelor of science degree at Michigan State Normal College in Ypsilanti, Michigan, in 1948. He was a teaching fellow at University of Michigan's Horace Rackham School of Education, where he received a master's degree in education. Advanced studies were completed at Central Michigan College.

His career as an educator included teaching industrial arts, general science, and audio-visual arts in Rapid River, Escanaba, and Alpena Public Schools. He also served as Director of the planetarium in Alpena. After his retirement from public education in 1977, he and Idamae volunteered for three years at Twin Wells Indian School in Sun Valley, Arizona.

Clifford was a regular contributor to *The Onaway Outlook* for more than 20 years. His columns started with "On the Road with Cliff and Idamae Roberts" followed by "Not on the Road," which became "From the Riverbank" after purchase of the home on Black River. Upon moving to Black Lake, his column became "From the Lakeshore."

He has four children (Bruce—1945, Ann—1948, Paul—1951, and Dale—1957), nine grandchildren, and seventeen great grandchildren. Idamae died in January 1994. Clifford married Florence Webster in December 1996, adding three more children and six more grandchildren. Clifford and Florence currently live on Hongore Bay, Black Lake, ten miles north of Onaway.

Name Index

Axford, Les, 90

Baker, George, 97
Ball, Rev. Charles, 239
Barnes, Nellie, 29, 30, 87
Barnett, I. J., 177
Beale, Billy, 25, 86
Bell, Alec, 210
Bell, Ann, 210
Bell, Cindy (Glawe), 210, 222
Bell, David, 210
Bell, Joshua, 210
Bell, Kristian, 210
Betker, Ryan, 210
Betker, Suzanne (Webster), 210
Bonner, Bob, 229
Bonner, Hod, 81
Bozman, Joel, 210
Braeutigam, Daniel, 210
Braeutigam, John, 210
Braeutigam, Laura Ann, 210
Braeutigam, Luke, 210
Braeutigam, Wendy (Glawe), 210
Breed, Bill, iii, xiii, xv
Brown, Roy, 103
Bruce, Dr., 84
Buckley, Donna, 239
Buehl, Clark, 86
Burden, Bert, 176
Buregard, R., 122
Butcher, Susan, 234

Butler, Miss Olive, 29
Bye, Harry, 84, 106

Carpenter, Dr., 37, 38
Chandler, Merritt, 241
Chapman, Pete, 142
Clemens, Fred, 102
Clifford, Rev., 238
Cryderman, Glen and Arlene, 178

Doane, Wm., 176
Doran, Jody, 16
Dosie, Miss Iva, 29
Downing, Trent, 189
Dunathon, Clint, 134
Dunn, Anna Munger, 204

Engle, Grace, 29
Evans, Jim and Hazel, 203, 206

Fairman, John, 20, 27, 36, 81, 158
Fairman, John and Adelia, 14, 37
Fairman, Nora, 13, 66
Faust, Robert, 122
Fitzpatrick, Clarissa, 121
Foster, Norman, 186
Francis, Bill and Ginger, 199
Francis, Joe, 176
Franklin, Meredith, 177
Freier, Orrin, 178

Gallo, Chris, 210
Gallo, Christopher, 210
Gallo, Jenny (Glawe), 210
Gallo, John, 210
Gallo, Richard, 210
Gallo, Sophie, 210
Gibbons, Euell, 98
Gillespie, Henry, 20
Glawe, Ann (Roberts), 170, 171, 207, 209, 210, 221, 222, 234, 242, 246, 249
Glawe, Dan, 171, 210, 221
Glover, G. F, 176
Gota, Miss Gertie, 176
Gota, Peter, 176
Goupell, Eddie, 75, 77, 82, 83, 106
Greene, Max and Dorothy, 202, 205
Gregg, Frank, 101
Gregg, Will and Mae, 101
Guinther, Ma, 84

Hamilton, Rev. John, 238
Hanchick, Mrs. Charles, 176
Hardy, Sally, 236, 248
Harmon, Mrs., 238
Hart, Pastor Fred, 238
Hatfield, Derek, 236
Hayner, Vera (Roberts), 33, 243
Hayner, William, 4
Henry, Charley, 6
Henry, Jim, 76
Hinson, Mary and John, 204
Hitzert, Russ, 26, 86

Hoffmeyer, Donnie, 155
Hosier, Sarah and Ernie, 194

Jackson, Vern, 8
Jarvis, Al and Zenie, 178
Jessup, Dave, 130
Jessup, Mary, 131

Kanjorski, Anton, 176
Kapalla, Edward, 4, 106, 180
Kapalla, Floyd, 30
Kapalla, Harry, 30
Kapalla, Kathleen, 4
Karr, Lewellyn, 104, 238
Karsten, Adolph, 178
King, Ralph, 77, 78
Koepsel, Roland, 106

Lamberson, Marcella and Lawerence, 120
Lamberson, Paula, 120
Lamberson, Puppet, 120
Landen, Clarence, 176
Lee, Jack, 106
Leffler, Arnold, 106
Leffler, Herb, 106
Leffler, Marvel, 106
Leopard, John, 25, 86
Light, Fred, 39
Little, Carmelita, 193
Lorentz, Wilbur and Judy, 193
Lound, Edna, 84, 160
Luke, David, 191
Lyon, Harriett, 186

MacGregor, Gilbert, 96
Malone, Harley, 6, 24
Mann, Billy, 158
Marquardt, Otto and Hilda, 200
Marshall, Albert, 176
Marshall, Bob, 70, 76, 179
Martin, Mrs., 9
Mather, Ward, 176
McClean, Mary and Dan, 234
McClellan, Elmer, 83
McClutchey, Carl, 106
McClutchey, Earl, 106
McClutchey, Ed, 65
McCormick, Bud, 106
McCormick, Earl, 106
McCormick, Maitland, 107
McCreery, Lee, 27, 28
McFall, Kenny, 97
McFall, Roger and Ruth, 97, 125, 196
McMillan, Dr., 47
McMullen, J. Edward, 176
McNeil, Dr., 11, 84
Mero, Charles, 4
Mero, Orem, 30
Merritt, Mike, 5, 29, 106
Minser, Charley, 97
Morrell, Virgil, 182

Nichol, Walter, 177
Nichols, Cody, 210
Noon, Doll, 106
Nye, Chester, 176

Phillips, Mrs. Emma, 177
Pierson, Rev., 53
Plower, Amelia, 177
Pokagon, Fern, 217
Porter, Kaye, 238
Potter, J. M., 14
Precour, Dorthy, 30
Precour, Eugene, 6
Pregitzer, Bob, 180
Pregitzer, Caroline, 155
Pregitzer, Karl, 43, 44

Quance, Velma, 177

Race, John, 51, 52, 64
Race, Mrs. John, 51
Riley, Roy, 7
Roberts, Adam, 210
Roberts, Arden, 16, 17, 33, 37, 55, 66, 69, 88, 90, 104, 243
Roberts, Bruce, iv, xiii, 54, 207, 209, 210, 221, 242, 246, 249
Roberts, Clarence, 72, 73, 79, 80, 90, 104, 107, 243
Roberts, Dale, 137, 170, 175, 207, 209, 210, 211, 221, 246, 249
Roberts, Earl, 23, 24, 27, 39, 51, 67, 68, 90
Roberts, Ella (Smith), 53
Roberts, Florence (Webster), xiii, 76, 119, 120, 121, 125, 187, 207, 228, 233, 234, 236, 238, 239, 248, 249
Roberts, Glen, 90

Roberts, Grace, 56
Roberts, Homer, 4, 19, 23, 27, 35, 39, 51, 52, 67, 104, 106, 178, 243
Roberts, Idamae (Lorentz), 40, 127, 132, 137, 170, 173, 176, 181, 182, 187, 188, 189, 191, 193, 194, 204, 206, 209, 211, 212, 219, 220, 223, 224, 226, 227, 238, 242, 246, 249
Roberts, Jack, 210
Roberts, Jeanine, 210
Roberts, Mr. and Mrs. John Sr., 56
Roberts, John Sr., 57
Roberts, John, 210
Roberts, Karen, xiii, 210
Roberts, Mark, 210
Roberts, Maybell, 1, 16, 51, 53, 57, 160, 238, 243, 244, 249
Roberts, Melissa, 210
Roberts, Oscar, 1, 2, 4, 16, 33, 53, 54, 57, 56, 57, 79, 158, 242, 243, 244, 249
Roberts, Paul, 148, 161, 170, 171, 207, 209, 210, 211, 221, 222, 246, 247, 249
Rosciam, Charlie, 39
Russell, Peter, 97

Sammond, Chloe, 210
Sammond, Chris, 210
Sammond, Erika (Roberts), 210
Sammond, Noah, 210
Sammond, Tony, 210

Schmidt, Harold, 233
Schmidt, Henry, 97
Schmidt, Ruth (Roberts), 33, 66, 243
Schoenhals, Glen, 49, 104
Scott, Andrew, 97
Shackson, Mr., 238
Shaw, Thomas, 241
Skinner, Ted, 167, 168, 178
Sloan, Kaye, 234
Smith, Bessie, 29
Smith, Bob, 106
Smith, Dorothy 234
Smith, Ed, 106
Smith, Frank, 107
Smith, Merl, 106
Smith, Vern, 170
Smock, Bob, 73
Smozzle, Ed, 108
Snody, Jim, 35, 102, 181
Snody, Phyllis, 181
Snogren, Rev. Dorraine, 239
Stark, Arthur, 4, 57
Stewart, Dr. Ken, 76, 233
Stout, Bud, 106
Strayer, Grant, 25

Thompson, Diane (Webster), 210, 239
Thompson, Trevor, 210
Tomkins, E. J., 177
Tucker, Dave, 86

Valley, Scrib, 65

Van Loon, Bill, 51
Van Zant, Walt, 97

Waggott, Helen, 121
Waldron, Jack and Nancy, 199
Warren, Beecher, 97
Webster, David, 210, 239
Webster, Eric, 125, 210
Webster, Katie, 125, 210
Webster, Lauren, 125, 210
Webster, Linda, 239
Webster, Steven, 210, 239
Webster, Trevor, 125, 210
Welch, Frank, 107
Wilkerson, Brianna, 210
Wilkerson, Bryce, 210
Wilkerson, David, 210
Wilkerson, Eve (Bozman), 210, 224
Willey, Dr., 84
Wilson, George, 79
Wilton, Bob, 121

Yeager, Mrs. David, 24, 110
Yeager, Perry, 111
Young, Annie, 9
Young, Miss Margaret, 28
Young, Pat, 104
Young, Ray, 89

Zarske, Carl, 177

Topical Index

Alpena, 14, 15, 47, 48, 109, 134, 135, 136, 153, 155, 158, 180, 207, 209, 210, 222, 238, 249
Alverno Dam, 166
Arizona, 188, 193, 201, 203, 204, 212, 217, 249
Arkansas, 193, 194
Army, xiii, 38, 209, 249
Ashes, 30, 226
Atlanta, 108, 109, 136
AuSable, 73
Avocado, 203, 206

Balloon, 103
Band, 31, 105, 106, 107
Bandit, 27, 28, 101
Barber, 39, 40, 226
Barber Bridge, 226
Bass, 67, 106, 107
Bell, 18, 86, 87, 102, 210
Big Fire, 6, 30, 111
Black Lake, xiii, 51, 62, 72, 75, 76, 82, 84, 115, 119, 120, 166, 179, 207, 210, 239, 249
Black River, xiii, 60, 115, 116, 119, 121, 125, 129, 137, 139, 145, 146, 164, 179, 207, 210, 224, 226, 249
Blacktop, 109
Boat, 33, 56, 130, 131, 132, 134, 135, 136, 137, 153

Boiler, 85, 108, 109
Bone marrow, 170, 171, 221
Bossy, 7, 9, 10, 11
Bread mixer, 99, 100
Bridge, 68, 125, 126, 155, 172, 190, 203, 226
Buck fever, 75

Cactus, 188, 203, 213
California, 187, 193, 200, 201, 202, 203, 204, 205, 206, 211
Camping, 72, 98, 129, 144, 193, 194, 199, 203, 211, 226
Campsite, 195, 201, 211
Canada, 57, 65, 142, 181, 187, 211, 238
CCC, 19, 104
Cemetery, 112, 113, 121
Cheboygan, 14, 20, 22, 56, 106, 107, 152, 172, 210, 238
China doll, 224, 225
Choir, 238, 239
Christmas, 60, 61, 62, 63, 90, 97, 144, 154, 161, 190, 191, 192, 197, 198, 219, 239
Church, 4, 39, 160, 172, 191, 192, 199, 200, 217, 218, 225, 238, 239
Circus, 23, 101
Clark Bridge, 226
Coal, 6, 16, 20, 21, 26, 96, 108

Cope Road, 158
County Normal, 19, 87, 249
Courthouse, 45, 47, 110, 186
Cribbage, 178, 193, 198, 204
Crockett Rapids, 142, 226

D & M, 14, 15, 16, 18, 20, 35, 49, 62, 67, 89, 97
Depot, 16, 17, 20, 22, 97
Depression, 2, 12, 18, 19, 90, 91, 96, 97
Desert, 201, 224
Dick, 6, 7, 8

Edna Lound's, 84, 160
Elderhostel, 184
Elevator, 1, 2, 4, 5, 6, 7, 8, 9, 10, 12, 13, 18, 20, 22, 23, 24, 25, 26, 31, 33, 35, 37, 57, 60, 82, 86, 89, 99, 100, 108, 113, 160, 183, 238
Ellenberger Hardware Store, 47
Erratt Bridge, 125
Escanaba, 134, 209, 249
Everling's, 81

Fairgrounds, 101, 102
Fishing, 51, 65, 67, 68, 69, 72, 73, 74, 75, 77, 115, 116, 117, 118, 130, 132, 134, 135, 136, 142, 182, 207
Florida, 21, 97, 161, 184, 195, 221
Fry bread, 216

Gage & Kramer Store, 13
Garage sale, 121
Gifts, 60, 61, 62, 219
Gladstone, 132
Glassies, 43, 44
Gumm's, 61, 180
Gyp, 25, 33, 79, 80, 83, 91

Halley's Comet, 149
Hankey Milling Co., 2, 4, 16, 24, 37, 45, 57, 113, 183
Harmon's Dry Goods Store, 53
Haunted house, 82
High Banks, 68, 69
Hobos, 18, 19
Hoeing, 26, 55
Homegoing, 223, 226
Homemade bread, 68, 86, 99, 100
Hoopstick, 41
Hopi, 218
Hospice, 236

Ice fishing, 75, 182
Ice out, 119, 120
Ice shanty, 77
Ideals, 31, 32

Johnson's Meat Market, 91

Lobdell, 6, 14, 30, 89
Loon, 51
Louisiana, 187, 189, 191, 192, 197
Lumber camp, 14, 90

Machinery, 4
Mahoney Lumber Co., 4
Maxon Field, 88
Megs, 43, 44
Merritt's Restaurant, 91
Michigan Rummy, 90, 91
Millersburg, 16, 17, 66
Mixer train, 16
Model T, 9, 10, 41, 64, 65, 66, 68, 205
Moltke, 178
Museum, 42, 106, 186, 201
Muskrats, 88
Muzzleloader, 82, 83

Navajo, 193, 215, 216, 217, 218

Oklahoma, 150, 193, 194

Peace Corps, 209, 211
Pete, the crow, 24
Petoskey, 2, 4, 209, 218
Philippines, 209, 211
Picnic, 16, 154, 171, 181, 223
Pigeon River, 144, 154, 226, 227
Pigs, 11, 23
Pike, 72, 74, 75, 77, 91, 118, 132
Pioneers, 90, 96, 238
Port Huron, 14, 65
Port Sanilac, 14
Posen, 67
Presque Isle, 16, 19, 67, 87, 108, 152, 176, 249

Rabbit, 27, 33, 60, 79, 80, 81, 82, 83, 91, 112, 132, 141, 144, 151, 162, 163, 164
Raccoon, 27, 28
Rapid River, 132, 134, 249
REPEAT, the crow, 25
Rototiller, 157
Rummy, 90, 91, 178, 198, 204

Salmon River, 130
Sandhill crane, 190
Saskatchewan, 57
Scarlet fever, 37
Sheep, 22, 23, 216
Show and tell, 17
Skating, 88
Skiing, 84, 85, 170, 181, 182, 184, 193
Skunk, 27, 49, 50, 157
Sledding, 84, 154
Slot machine, 101
Small pox, 37
Smelt, 121, 122, 132, 133, 179
Snody Drug Store, 35
Spitzer, 178, 204
Stark's elevator, 57
State Park, 189, 190, 191, 197, 199, 200, 201
Suckers, 68, 69, 74, 101, 132, 206

Teacher, xiii, xv, 5, 28, 29, 30, 87, 104, 132, 155, 178, 212, 238, 239

Texas, 71, 187, 189, 192, 193, 194, 197, 198, 199, 200, 206
Tomahawk Flooding, 154, 171
Tower, 14, 67, 88, 125, 126, 167, 177
Trail Tales, 54
Trains, xiii, 14, 15, 16, 20, 21, 205, 219
Tweed, 134, 135, 136, 137
Twin Wells, 193, 194, 202, 211, 212, 213, 214, 215, 217, 249

Walleye, 72, 132
Watermelon, 22
Weasel, 60, 61
Wood, 6, 10, 15, 41, 68, 70, 86, 90, 96, 99, 118, 144, 153, 161, 181, 183, 199, 216, 219, 224
Woodshed, 10, 36, 153, 183
Wright's Newsery, 26, 43, 49
WWII, 19

978-0-595-50836-5
0-595-50836-7